ROUTLEDGE LIBRARY EDITIONS:
POLITICAL PROTEST

Volume 10

THE GERMAN PEASANT WAR OF 1525

THE GERMAN PEASANT WAR OF 1525

Edited by
JANOS BAK

LONDON AND NEW YORK

First published in 1976 by Frank Cass & Co. Ltd.

This edition first published in 2022
by Routledge
2 Park Square, Milton Park, Abingdon, Oxon OX14 4RN

and by Routledge
605 Third Avenue, New York, NY 10158

Routledge is an imprint of the Taylor & Francis Group, an informa business

© 1976 Frank Cass & Co. Ltd.

All rights reserved. No part of this book may be reprinted or reproduced or utilised in any form or by any electronic, mechanical, or other means, now known or hereafter invented, including photocopying and recording, or in any information storage or retrieval system, without permission in writing from the publishers.

Trademark notice: Product or corporate names may be trademarks or registered trademarks, and are used only for identification and explanation without intent to infringe.

British Library Cataloguing in Publication Data
A catalogue record for this book is available from the British Library

ISBN: 978-1-03-203038-8 (Set)
ISBN: 978-1-00-319086-8 (Set) (ebk)
ISBN: 978-1-03-204209-1 (Volume 10) (hbk)
ISBN: 978-1-03-204210-7 (Volume 10) (pbk)
ISBN: 978-1-00-319095-0 (Volume 10) (ebk)

DOI: 10.4324/9781003190950

Publisher's Note
The publisher has gone to great lengths to ensure the quality of this reprint but points out that some imperfections in the original copies may be apparent.

Disclaimer
The publisher has made every effort to trace copyright holders and would welcome correspondence from those they have been unable to trace.

The German Peasant War of 1525

Edited by
JANOS BAK

Routledge
Taylor & Francis Group
New York   London

First published by FRANK CASS & CO. LTD.

This edition published 2013 by Routledge

711 Third Avenue, New York, NY 10017
2 Park Square, Milton Park, Abingdon, Oxon OX14 4RN

Routledge is an imprint of the Taylor & Francis Group, an informa business

Copyright © 1976 Frank Cass & Co. Ltd.

ISBN 0 7146 3063 2

This group of studies first appeared in a Special Issue on The German Peasant War of 1525 of *The Journal of Peasant Studies*, Volume 3 No. 1, published by Frank Cass and Company Limited.

All rights reserved. No part of this publication may be reproduced in any form or by any means, electronic, mechanical, photocopying, recording or otherwise, without the prior permission of the publishers

Contents

Editors' Introduction	vii
Sketch Map of the German Peasant War	viii
From Resistance to Revolt: The Late Medieval Peasant Wars in the Context of Social Crisis **František Graus**	1
The Peasants of Swabia, 1525 **Henry J. Cohn**	10
Images of the Peasant, 1514–1525 **R. W. Scribner**	29
Precursors of the Peasant War: *Bundschuh* and *Armer Konrad*—Movements at the Eve of the Reformation **Adolf Laube**	49
'Old Law' and 'Divine Law' in the German Peasant War **Heide Wunder**	54
The Economic, Social and Political Background of the Twelve Articles of the Swabian Peasants of 1525 **Peter Blickle**	63
German Agrarian Insitutions at the Beginning of the Sixteenth Century: Upper Swabia as an Example **David Sabean**	76
'The Peasant War in Germany' by Friedrich Engels—125 Years After **Janos Bak—Rainer Wohlfeil—Ernst Engelberg—Günter Vogler—Edward Friedman Kurt Greussing and Hans G. Kippenberg**	89

Editors' Introduction

The immense importance of the German Peasant War, both in itself as the first national peasant revolt in Germany and because of the influence of Engels' work on the subject, hardly needs to be emphasized here. When Janos Bak suggested the possibility of a special number of the *Journal of Peasant Studies* on the War, in this the 450th anniversary year, we accepted his idea with alacrity. Janos Bak has taken responsibility for the issue as guest-editor and we are most grateful to him for the imagination, skill, and careful hard work with which he has prepared it. He, in his turn, wishes to acknowledge the help of his friend, Dr. Edward J. Hundert.

One of our contributors remarks that he was 'struck by the similarities between the Swabian peasants of 1525 in their organization, demands and action and those that occurred under Zapata in the heart of Mexico during the second decade of the twentieth century, as outlined by Eric Wolf' (Benecke). The comparison is an intriguing one. We believe that our readers will find others which are no less fascinating.

EDITORS, *The Journal of Peasant Studies*

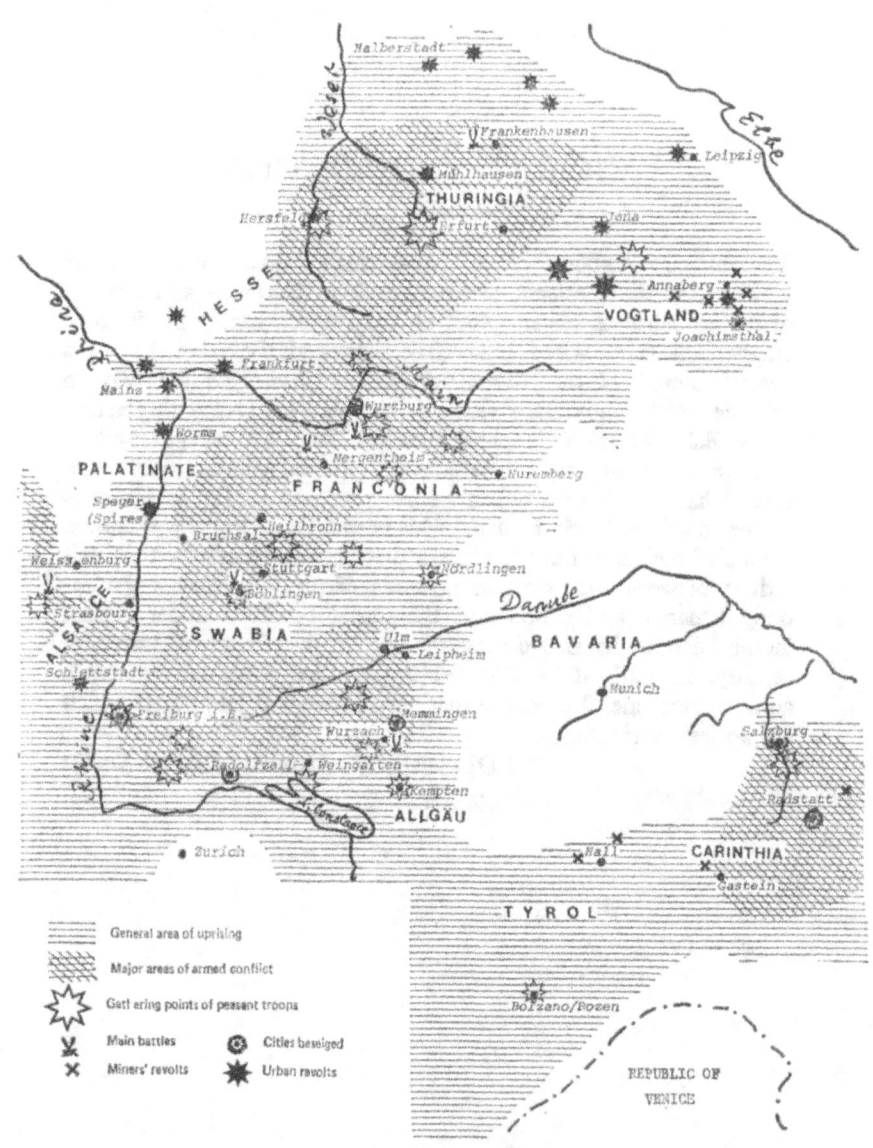

SKETCH MAP OF THE GERMAN PEASANT WAR 1524–1526
(adapted from G. Vogler, *Die Gewalt soll gegeben werden dem gemeinen Volk*, Berlin 1975)
(Scale and size of symbols have not been rigorously observed)

From Resistance to Revolt: The Late Medieval Peasant Wars in the Context of Social Crisis

František Graus[*]

This study offers an overview of the growth of peasant resistance from the early Middle Ages into the sixteenth century. Touching upon major questions of the ideology and organization of the Peasant War and its predecessors, it serves as an introduction to the problems to which this special issue is devoted. The author registers the recurrent waves of peasant resistance throughout the medieval centuries but stresses the novel qualities of the late medieval ones, beginning with the English rising of 1381, through the Hussites to the Peasant War of 1525. In particular, the mature ideological formulations and the innovative forms of organization and propaganda were the signs of a new type of movement. The defeat of the peasants was not without consequences: it served as one of the factors in the emergence of the early modern state.

The image of the medieval centuries as exclusively dark ages has now been followed into oblivion by that other one which depicted the Middle Ages as an idyllic period in which every man was content with the state 'to which the Lord had called him'. Recent historical research has convincingly demonstrated that the so-called Middle Ages were characterized by recurrent conflicts in the countryside and later in the cities as well. If the alleged social harmony of this age existed at all, it probably did so only in the limited social circles where men did not have to earn their daily bread by hard labour. Learned divines confirmed that it was ordained that most of the people should labour; the majority worked hard and upon them, the despised *rustici*, fell the burden of feeding the entire society. Medieval peasants were not always content with their assigned place and occasionally resisted their fate. The rural struggles that resulted from these outbursts did not, however, add up to a continuous series of revolts, for throughout the centuries the evidence for them is very uneven. There are periods of obvious upswing in these struggles, while other decades seem to have been very peaceful indeed, with little significant evidence of resistance to be found.

A comparison of the peasant movements of the Middle Ages with those of modern Europe does not have to raise the question of the existence of revolts in the earlier period. This has been answered affirmatively long

[*] *Professor of History at the University of Basel (Switzerland). This text has been translated from the German.*

ago. The questions that have to be raised and studied are the following: (1) What actions of medieval peasants are to be judged as acts of resistance? (2) When and why do these struggles increase and which are the historical periods and geographic areas of particularly active resistance? and (3) What are the characteristic features of the great late medieval revolts? Finally, one may add the concomitant question: What was the reaction of the lords to the growth of peasant revolt and resistance?

If the authors of penitentials and medieval sermons can be trusted, the most frequent cardinal sins to which the peasants succumbed were cheating on the tithe (or outright refusal to render the ecclesiastical dues), theft (particularly ploughing into their neighbour's field), laxity in faith and intemperance in food and drink. Although lack of devotion and gluttony were censored in all social classes, it comes as no surprise to discover that people who lived virtually always on the verge of starvation availed themselves of every feast to eat their fill. Characteristically, the utopian ideal of those who had to worry about their daily bread was the vision of *Schlaraffenland*, a place where food grew without toil and fried pigeons flew into one's mouth (as is so splendidly depicted by Pieter Brueghel). However, refusal to pay the tithe and the various forms of theft are clearly acts of passive resistance. The forms of these were so varied and our sources so inconclusive that it is hardly possible to decide in individual cases whether a peasant was indeed so impoverished (perhaps because of bad harvest or pillage) that he was unable to pay his dues or whether he followed age-old tradition and just complained about his poverty in order to avoid paying them. Precisely because these forms of 'resistance' were so tempting and also so volatile and elusive, the accused could rarely be proved to be in the wrong. Therefore, they remained very popular with the peasants well beyond the Middle Ages. Similarly vague were the charges in matters of faith. That peculiar mixture of medieval popular piety which contained pagan elements as well as the belief in the mystical healing and protective power of the sacraments, was certainly somewhat contrary to the official teachings of the church. Open heresy was rare in the countryside, and it was rather this pagan-Christian alloy, combined with a basic distrust for the clergy that characterized peasant attitudes to the church. The 'laxity of faith' that medieval preachers did not tire of denouncing throughout the centuries—apparently with little success—referred to this type of unorthodoxy.

Besides these kinds of passive, 'stubborn', peasant behaviour there is also ample evidence of widespread active resistance, mainly in the form of individual rebellion. These acts were registered as 'sins' in the penitentials and subsumed under 'theft'. The wording of ecclesiastical censures suggests that medieval rural people regarded it as perfectly acceptable to help oneself to seigneurial property, if only one was not caught. The most frequent forms of 'theft', poaching and illegal felling of trees, were cruelly punished by the lords. Arson, the revenge of the powerless, was also widespread. Armed resistance against the rich, reflected in the new literary figure of the Robin

Hood style of bandit (the medieval variant of the ancient type of the noble robber), can be seen as a transition from the anarchic, individual action to collective resistance. This is quite obvious, for instance, in the case of Wilhelm Tell, who was actually a hunter and shepherd but came to be regarded as the leader and hero of the common struggle of Swiss peasants. The medieval 'primitive rebel' acted as an individual, but several lonely outlaws could form a group, outside settled society, and wage their war against the rich. They could not sustain their feud with the established order unless they could count on the sympathy of the oppressed and obtain steady assistance from them. When the rebels were able to sweep along considerable numbers of the population beyond passive support, we witness open peasant rebellions.

Rural uprisings occasionally reached considerable size and spread like prairie-fire. Our earliest example of such open resistance dates from 841 A.D. when Saxon peasants are reported to have risen against their lords in the so-called Stellinga rebellion. There is evidence of similar events in late tenth century Normandy but by the eleventh century after the uprisings in Poland and around Novgorod such large scale movements seem to have ceased. The records of the following centuries are silent about rebellions, though minor conflicts and riots are mentioned in every part of Europe. In the later Middle Ages revolts again develop into greater uprisings: in the fourteenth century peasants took up arms in Flanders, France and England; in the fifteenth century Bohemia was the centre of extended struggles, and the sixteenth century opened with peasant wars in Hungary and southern Germany, to name only the best known.

Beyond and above these open revolts, the chronology of which is certainly not accidental, careful analysis can detect regional concentrations of passive resistance that often preceded and prepared the way for greater revolts. A good example of an area where frequent minor riots and confrontations led to major revolts and finally to the great peasant war of 1525 is the Alsace and the Upper Rhineland. The factors that made this territory into a hot-bed of unrest can be clearly identified (see below, pp. 66 ff., 81 ff.).

The forms, dates and places of peasant resistance lead up logically to the second question about the causes and conditions of the escalation from isolated incidents to peasant revolt. Peasant life in 'normal times' was hard enough. The low yields of medieval agriculture meant that a bad harvest could cause serious famine. The continuous wars and feuds hit the peasant most. The yeoman and serf were at their lord's mercy and whim at all times. Not only was the 'rustic' mistreated by all, he was also despised, even by those wandering scholars who, while mocking him, pestered him for alms. All this, however, belonged to the daily routine of peasant life and only an unusually sharp increase of pressure could trigger a reaction of despair, such as the desperate response of the French Jacquerie in 1358. It seems to have been a rule that a particularly striking event was needed to make the proverbial bitter cup run over. For example, the Pastoureux uprising of 1251, a very strange movement which remained essentially incomprehensible even to contemporaries, was started by a rumour about the capture of the king by the infidel. Similarly, the English revolt of 1381 got its immediate impetus from the levy of a special tax. Pogroms against the Jews are another typical example of such spontaneous, violent reactions to unforeseen or incomprehensible events such as the Black Death.

It is remarkable that many medieval authors, even those not particularly sensitive to the plight of the peasants, notice a high irritability among the people of the countryside. This oversensitivity often caused highly exaggerated reactions to relatively trivial events: cause and consequence were frequently out of proportion. However, in all those movements that went beyond local riots and revolts there are definite signs that the entire set of social values was shaken. These crises were mostly articulated in a demand for justice, because the existing order did not seem to be 'normal' (i.e., just) and redress was urgently needed. The great wave of revolts in the ninth to eleventh centuries from Normandy to Novgorod were obviously motivated by resistance against feudal subjection by peasants who had been able to retain their old 'freedom', in these peripheral regions much longer than elsewhere. In the second and much more extensive revolutionary wave of the late Middle Ages the peasants—their freedom long since lost—found themselves at an increasing economic disadvantage because of the so called agrarian crisis. Moreover, they began to realize that their servile status was not, as their forbears tended to believe, the result of 'divine will'. The assumption had first been discredited by learned theologians, who were promptly declared heretical. But the idea spread quickly. John Ball's famous sermons raised the question of whence the nobility came; the Taborites made divine justice their basic standard and the radical wing of Hussites reached the point of denying the legitimacy of lordship over any Christian. Divine justice became the battle cry of the German Peasant War, and this 'ideological basis' enabled the peasants to go beyond fighting for the special grievances of their particular communities and start a struggle for a new order established according to God's will and justice (see below p. 54 ff.).

While taking the crucial step of ideological justification, the late medieval peasant rebels also discovered the importance of organization. Before the fifteenth century revolts had remained isolated or, at best, had spread 'snow-ball' fashion (e.g., the Jacquerie). As long as the enemy had little power, or there were such enemies as the urban Jews who had no power at all, the weakness of peasant organization did not become apparent. Other movements grew in the shadow of higher social groups which supplied the leadership. This was so in the Crusades in which at first (1095-99) the poor had played a quite important part, but not that of organizers. The task of efficient organization became urgent as soon as the peasants alone confronted their enemies.

A consciously built organization appeared first, perhaps, in the Great Society of 1381, definitely with the Hussites, and with greater clarity in the German Peasant War and its immediate predecessors (*Bundschuh, Armer Konrad,* see below, p. 49 ff.). However, the early examples already pointed to the shortcomings of peasant forms of organization. When a single defeat is enough to seal the fate of an entire uprising, the structure of the struggle is obviously weak. The Hussites alone were an exception in this respect, but only as long as their fight was carried on by a coalition of rural poor, cities and minor nobles. Although the village community, grown out of economic and technological necessity, acquired considerable legal, social and even spiritual functions, this did not add up to a viable basis for more general action. While it was able to protect its individual members from seigneurial or judicial rancor, the village as a unit almost invariably failed as a nucleus of more widely based movements.

A major question of both ideological and organizational nature was the identification of the main enemy. There were plenty of enemies to choose from. Despised and maltreated by all, medieval peasants mistrusted and disliked everyone: the bailiffs, the tax-collectors, the burghers, whom they suspected of cheating them, and the priests, whom they would not trust with their dogs but on whom they had to rely for salvation. Of course, this was nothing like a genuine 'class consciousness' and the actual owner of the land was often too far away to be recognized as the real enemy. The country gentry, the freeholder or the *Ritter* was likely to be perceived as the primary adversary. However, he may have also been considered a possible ally or even—at least for the wealthier peasants—a model to follow. But it was usually the bailiff, the priest and especially the abbot's man (on the most efficiently run monastic estates) whom the peasants met day by day and whose immediate power oppressed them. Hence the abuse of lordship appeared to be the most hateful thing, more than lordship itself. Lordship *per se,* particularly that symbolized by the person of the king, was not only accepted without challenge, but remained a part of the peasants' naive belief in the right order of the world. (The Hussites in this respect, once again, proved to be exceptional in discarding the notion of the good king corrupted by evil counsellors). Enmity and hatred were thus focused on those who could be charged with 'illegal lordship': the stewards of the seigneurs, the beadles and bailiffs and, particularly from the fourteenth century onwards, the clergy, whose secular power was bitterly resented and felt to be a sin against divine justice.

The peasants' intuitive discovery of the force of organization and their questioning of the legality of at least some aspects of dominion brings us to our third question. There can be no doubt that during the fourteenth to sixteenth centuries peasant revolts not only increased in number and frequency, but also became more extensive and more radical, and it is important to examine the characteristic features of the upsurge. The roots lay in the economic conditions caused by the difficulties of the agrarian economy in late medieval Europe. The fall of grain prices increased seigneurial pressure on the peasants as the lords attempted to raise their shrinking income by the increase of dues and by new exactments. The agrarian crisis was accompanied by higher prices for urban manufactured goods and by the manifold tribulations of war and pillage. In Central Europe mercenaries such as the infamous Armagnacs, ruthlessly exploited the peasants, owing to the fact that the troops were most likely insufficiently supplied and thus forced to live off the land. Money lost its value at an ever increasing rate since the lords of the mints found coin debasement still the quickest and easiest source of income. Mercenary armies had to be paid and so taxation was re-discovered in almost all European principalities. The ever-increasing burden of these demands had to be shouldered by the 'third estate': the peasants and the townspeople (see below, p. 50). There was plenty of social gunpowder around that could be lit by the fuse of any minor conflict, nor was there any lack of such events.

In earlier centuries all this would have probably caused only local riots and regional rebellions. The extensive peasant wars of the late Middle Ages have to be explained by additional factors. One of these was the appearance and wide acceptance of an ideological basis. First there were the doubts about the divine sanction for clerical authority. Demands for the justification of the priestly office by exemplary moral conduct were as old as the Church itself, and had been denounced as heretical at least since the fourth century. A step beyond the refusal to accept an unworthy cleric was to question the worthiness of the clergy in general and to contrast the poverty of Christ with the riches of the lords spiritual. The Great Schism (1396-1416), during which popes excommunicated each other and abused their opponents' followers, gave wide publicity to the problems in Christianity. Simultaneously the Bible became more widely available through translation into the vernacular and came to be the measure of all things. According to Scripture, even in its official interpretation, men were equal—a harsh contrast to late medieval social reality.

More significant still was that the questioning is of clerical authority affected the force and validity of the sacraments. These rites which hitherto served, with all their formalities, as safe refuge from over-towering dangers, might lose their power if administered by an unchaste and sinful priest: there seemed to be no security and no shelter any more. True, such articulate ideas were only in the minds of a few, but contemporary evidence suggests that a great number of simple people had a feeling of insecurity and a fear of some undefined threat. As early as the Hussite movement (1419-34) these ideas were clearly formulated and put into writing in the Four Prague Articles. The chalice, symbolizing the claim of the laity to full participation in the sacrament of the altar, became a widely understood sign for a new kind of security in the proximity of God. Communion in both kinds (bread and wine) promised a reliable sacrament permitting every Christian to freely seek the divine truth of the Gospel and fight for the abolition of a sinful world. The Hussites consistently denounced and attacked the secular power of the Church. Henceforth the contrast between the Biblical command of poverty and the reality of ecclesiastical dominion was not just discussed by small secret groups of 'heretics': such matters were preached about from the pulpit and taught in public. No wonder that the official hierarchy was frightened by the spread of these ideas.

The Hussite Revolution did not put forward explicit peasant demands. Their outlook remained biblical-theological and the next major step in the formulation of a specific programme was not taken until the German Peasant War. Now, for the first time, the peasants' demands were articulated in a general form together with particular and local grievances. The first signs of a 'de-theologization' of the language and the contents can be detected in the articles and manifestoes of 1524-26 (see below, p. 10 ff.). Nevertheless, the success of both was limited. The Hussites were isolated as 'heretics' by the Church, which managed to equate Czech and Hussite with heterodoxy in the minds of fifteenth century men. The German Peasant War was crushed ruthlessly, and it was to be a long time before peasant demands could be re-formulated. No programme of the great peasant revolts of early modern Europe surpassed the Twelve Articles, indicating that the 1525 formulation remained valid for quite some time.

The late medieval peasant revolts also signify a new epoch in the organizational forms of rebellion. Here again a high point was reached that could not be surpassed for centuries. Unions and alliances—such as the urban and knightly leagues—became widespread in the late Middle Ages. (The Swiss Confederation, founded in the late thirteenth century, had relatively little impact owing to the very special conditions—geographical and otherwise—of the Alpine valleys, although their existence was often cited by the authorities as a dangerous example.) The Hussites developed the most mature organizations, no doubt because their movement could count, besides peasants, many knights and a great number of cities as leading forces. Thus they could avail themselves of tested examples and experienced men, and were also able to introduce new forms. The usual medium of propaganda, the sermon, was augmented by songs (*cantilena*) and pictures. Through images Biblical commands could be convincingly contrasted with ecclesiastical reality; the church song proved to be so impressive and popular that it was to become a basis of a new order in the army. The Hussites won their greatest victories with their innovative tactics, the war waggons, based on a new structure of the army and essentially stemming from peasant experience and mentality.

In the German Peasant War the preparatory stage was not as in Bohemia, the work of clerics and preachers, but of peasant and urban propagandists. The Hussite organizational forms could not simply be transplanted because the German peasants, as a rule, lacked the allies with military experience, the minor nobility. However, they had a new weapon which the Hussites had not yet been able to wield: their friends and supporters could use the recent invention of the printing press for the mass production of leaflets and pamphlets (see below, pp. 29 ff.). These broadsheets and other printed matter became a forceful means of propaganda as early as the 1500s, although, the enemies of the peasants used it with no less—and finally with greater—success.

In short, during the late Middle Ages we see the reception of different forms of organization by peasant movements and the realization of the importance of preparation and propaganda, but not the solution to the problem of keeping events under control in the rural, village-bound environment. This major shortcoming seems to have been inevitable. Although everything experienced in the life beyond the pale of the village suggested convincingly the necessity of organization and association, its realization encountered great objective and subjective obstacles in the rural environment. Except during the depth of winter (which, however, was a bad time for revolts) the peasants were bound throughout the year to their fields and villages, perhaps more by the needs of cultivation than by the demand of the lords. Only if tillage was abandoned, as the Taborites proposed in their early, radical phase, could these fetters of localism be broken. A temporary break for field work proved always to be a hindrance to action. Also, the enemy was often perceived only in a vague and frequently incorrect way; the discussion above about the 'illegitimate use' of lordship as the source of injustice rather than lordship itself indicates this very well. The *misuse* of power was seen to lead to the oppression of the poor and the luxury of the rich. Hence luxury itself became the immediately perceived object of the struggle, riches were destroyed or pillaged, and thus many an uprising tended to disintegrate into looting. Another serious limitation was the belief in the good ruler who would intervene if only he knew how badly off his subjects were. This paradigm, present already in 1381 (and even before), remained in different variations characteristic of peasant revolts well into our own times.

The unity of the village was frequently endangered from within. Tenants of different lords often fought with each other over economic disputes, such as rights of common pasture. Social antagonism within the village community began to become apparent as well. Production for the market fostered social differentiation, which had its roots in much earlier times. Although the great losses of life in the plague of the late fourteenth century caused a temporary shortage of labour in the countryside and a sharp increase in agricultural wages, this equalising process was soon over and social tensions increased again in the fifteenth century. The lack of military experience, however, proved to be the most decisive factor in all these wars. With very few exceptions, peasants were no longer arms-bearing; they had no up-to-date weapons and were rarely able to wield the old ones. Their military experience, if it can be called that, was merely passive, as victims of feudal and mercenary campaigns. True, military technology had not yet progressed so far that a straight scythe or a nailed flail could not have served as an impressive weapon, but a troop equipped with such poor arms had to be led by a tactical genius if it was to have any chance against the lords, as Žižka showed in the early, victorious period of the Hussite wars. The peasants were well aware of the need for trained and experienced military leadership: and many of the rebels tried to enlist knights as commanders even if they had to be coerced into accepting the commissions.

The popularity of deserting mercenaries, who occasionally joined ranks with the rural poor, stems from the same need. In the last resort, the lords had all the advantages on their side, even against the genuine great peasant uprisings (again, with the exception of the Hussites).

Still, the lessons of the peasant wars of the late Middle Ages were not entirely lost on the victorious lords. They realized that against the individual rebel or a few rioting villages one lord, maybe with the help of his neighbours, could be easily successful, but against the great revolts which hit like a hurricane they could not stand alone. They also realized that new forms of organization were needed, and the experience of the great uprisings was one of the reasons—though certainly not the only one—for the strengthening of the central authority, the state. The late Middle Ages are commonly regarded as the birthdate of the modern state in its different forms and variations. In Western Europe the first elements of absolute monarchy emerge; in Central Europe the outlines of territorial principalities are drawn.

The upheavals of the fourteenth to sixteenth centuries, which have often been called by the handy but equivocal term 'crisis', demonstrated many of the limits of the contemporary conditions and led through the revolts and uprisings to significant dislocations. A solution to the conflicts in the countryside could not be found, but in many respects—in technology, economy and also in social consciousness—these centuries mark a high point that was not to be surpassed for many generations. The most consequential immediate result of the upheavals was the growth of modern states, which defined a new and wider space for the events and struggles to come.

In this sense the late medieval centuries did witness a 'crisis' of the old society and at the same time an upsurge in revolts greater than ever before which led to the developments in ideology and organization. Not a few of these novel elements are still significant for social movements both in Europe and elsewhere.

NOTE

Specific references to the single problems of this article would amount to an extensive critical bibliography. The reader is referred to the author's survey in 'Das Spätmittelalter als Krisenzeit. Ein Literaturbericht als Zwischenbilanz', *Mediaevalia Bohemica* (1969) Suppl. 1–75. Among the more recent publications the excellent summary of peasant resistance up to and including the English revolt of 1381 by Rodney Hilton, *Bond Men Made Free* (London, 1974) and the book by Jozef Macek, *Jean Hus et les traditions hussites* (Paris, 1973) may be mentioned. The numerous publications of the last few years on the German peasant war of 1525 and its period are referred to in the articles in this issue, cf. especially pp. 133–135.

The Peasants of Swabia, 1525

Henry J. Cohn*

What peasants felt about their condition and how they proposed that it should be remedied emerged more clearly in the German Peasants' War than in any other pre-industrial popular movement. The hundreds of surviving lists of peasant articles were compiled in some respects like the *cahiers* of the French Revolution, but only in a few cases were they profoundly changed or reworded by the more educated and socially elevated leaders who put them to paper. The form and content of these complaints varied: some were as generalized as the Twelve Articles of the peasants of Upper Swabia which gained wide currency throughout Germany; others were the more particular complaints by the subjects of one overlord or in a single village; and yet others were the protests of individual peasants like the 400 submissions made by subjects of the prince-abbot of Kempten. Given the considerable variety and the great length and intricate detail of many of these *gravamina*, the Twelve Articles and several other relatively concise examples, drawn from Swabia and adjacent lands, may be taken as representative of the kind of grievances expressed also—though with variations—in Alsace, the Rhineland, Württemberg, the Black Forest, Thuringia, Franconia, Salzburg, the Tirol, Switzerland and elsewhere. Swabia not only provides the greatest variety of sources of quotable length, but in the history of the Peasants' War, it was the region where, in the first months of 1525, the revolt gathered momentum after the initial hesitations in the original Black Forest rising at the end of 1524. Moreover, it was following the Swabian example and usually inspired by the Twelve Articles that many other regions in Germany and beyond its frontiers joined the rising during the ensuing months.

The Twelve Articles (document I) were compiled in the town of Memmingen between 27 February and 1 March 1525 by Sebastian Lotzer, a journeyman furrier who was a Lutheran pamphleteer and lay preacher. Lotzer was scribe not only for the representatives of 27 villages subject to Memmingen, but of the Baltringen troop of 7,000 or more rebellious peasants north of Memmingen towards Ulm. On 16 February some 300 lists of articles had been presented by the Baltringen peasants to the Swabian League of lay and ecclesiastical princes, nobles and cities; document II, with its typical grammatical errors and repetition of stock phrases, is one of over 30 of these Baltringen complaints still extant. From the Baltringen articles Lotzer extracted the chief heads into the Twelve Articles, at the same time as he drafted 11 articles in similar terms for the Memmingen

---

Senior Lecturer, Department of History, University of Warwick.

peasants. Unlike many of the Baltringen articles, which concentrated largely on the reduction of dues and services to previous levels, the Twelve Articles put all the issues at stake between lords and peasants to the touchstone of God's Word as expressed in the Scriptures. Some of the 60 biblical references in the margins (not printed below), as well as the justificatory introduction, were added by Christoph Schappeler, the Zwinglian preacher who had railled against tithes at Memmingen since 1523 [*Franz, 1969: 118-27; 1936 : 193-213*].

The Twelve Articles were an outline blueprint for the reform of agrarian society. The Baltringen peasants had decided on 27 February that reform was to be worked out in detail on the advice of men learned in Scripture. Not ancient custom, but divine law was the criterion of what they would accept. The Twelve Articles made far-reaching demands, based on the Gospel, for elected priests, evangelical preaching, reallocation of the tithes, and the abolition of serfdom and heriots. A more moderate disposition was shown in asking for the reduction, not abolition, of rents, services and fines and in proposing a measure of compromise over the commons and forests. Inequalities of wealth would have been preserved and government and authority upheld. Yet the net effect of implementing the Twelve Articles would have been a fundamental shift in economic power and social status in favour of the lower orders and at the expense of the lords. The extent of village autonomy in local matters would have been enhanced. God's Word and brotherly love were envisaged as the principles of justice which would have prevented any future reversal of the balance in favour of the lords.

The Twelve Articles, printed within three weeks, were soon taken over verbatim by peasants in many parts of Germany, even in places where some of the complaints did not apply, as in Thuringia which had little serfdom. Elsewhere the Twelve Articles formed the basis for other sets of articles which added to or subtracted from them to meet local circumstances. Even in Upper Swabia, the two other troops who joined together with the Baltringer in the Christian Union at the beginning of March did not adopt the Twelve Articles. The Lake of Constance troop, south-west of Memmingen, adopted 12 articles drawn up at Rappertsweiler, fewer than half of which corresponded to those compiled by Lotzer; the main difference in emphasis lay in the exercise of fair justice by elected judges. The Allgäu troop, south-east of Memmingen, seems to have adopted the Rappertsweiler articles in June, but earlier an extremely anti-clerical group of articles was current in this area (document III). Indeed Wilhelm Rem, a Lutheran chronicler at Augsburg, gave these general articles and not the Twelve Articles as those of the Swabian rebels. They were likewise entitled simply 'The Articles of the rebellious peasants in Germany' by the inveterate Venetian diarist, Marino Sanuto; his version, fuller and slightly different from Rem's, also survives in two variant Italian manuscripts in the archives at Brescia [*Roth, 1896 : 221-3; Sanuto, 1893, vol. 38 : cols. 244-6; Guerrini, 1947 : 292-3*]. The first five of these articles betray Lutheran or Zwinglian influences in insisting on the good conduct of the lower clergy and monks. The next five launch a powerful attack on the political and economic might of especially the higher clergy and monasteries.

Anti-clericalism of this nature was widespread in most of the major areas of revolt and reappeared, for instance, in the articles of the Salzburg and Tirolese peasants. With only a few exceptions, clerical lords were the first and main object of attack by the rebels in 1525, as they had been during the wave of preliminary risings between 1431 and 1517. During almost this entire period the peasants subject to the abbots of Kempten in the Allgäu had engaged in a running battle with successive prelates who forced free peasants and half-free *Zinser* to become their serfs. The first Kempten rising of 1491 had already broached the themes that would recur in 1525: high military taxation, restrictions on marriage, reduction in status, confiscation of inheritances, and attempts to replace hereditary by life tenure of land, all enforced by grievous arbitrary imprisonment, excessive fines and chancery fees, and ecclesiastical penalties [Blickle, 1973 : 319-20]. The abbots ignored even the slight concessions made to the peasants in 1492; repeated negotiations before representatives of the Swabian League since 1523 proved fruitless against an obdurate abbot. The desperate peasants collected 400 depositions listing the misfortunes which some 1,200 of their number had met at the hands of their lords since 1492 (for examples, see document IV). Not surprisingly, it was the Kempten peasants who first raised the standard of revolt in the Allgäu in 1525, to be joined soon by the subjects of the bishop of Augsburg and other ecclesiastical and lay lords.

Schedules of grievances are the most important sources emanating from the peasants themselves in 1525, but by no means the only ones. Besides numerous confessions extracted from captured rebels, there is an abundance of correspondence sent out by peasant chanceries, treaties made among themselves or with the lords, and ordinances issued for their own discipline and to control the areas they occupied. A common practice was to form a Christian alliance or brotherhood for the fourfold purpose of recruiting adherents, presenting a united front against lords, conducting military operations, and implementing the desired reforms. The three troops of Upper Swabian rebels whose representatives met at Memmingen at the beginning of March had difficulty in agreeing on how permanent their Christian Union should be and how much centralized control should be exercised over the separate regions [Buszello, 1969 : 58-67; Sabean, 1972 : 11-13; Franz 1969 : 127-8]. The form of alliance eventually adopted, first by the Allgäu troop on 7 March (document V) and three days later by the others with minor changes, was more of a loosely coordinated interim arrangement for administering the areas their forces occupied than a permanent and tightly controlled league designed to last beyond the expected reformation of society, such as the Baltringen troop had proposed. Nevertheless, this league of peasants, originally devised along the lines of contemporary leagues of knights or the first Swiss peasant leagues, was still clearly intended as a counterweight to the Swabian League of lords and as an institution which might ensure, by force if necessary, that divine law would govern future relationships between lords and peasants. Castles and monasteries were to be neutralized, and the princes and lords deprived of officials and garrisons who might serve them against the peasants. Restrictions were placed on craftsmen and mercenary soldiers. The measures for an elected hierarchy and military discipline within the league were supplemented by other ordinances issued at this time which drew upon both the experience of village self-government and the military practices of the ex-soldiers (*Landsknechte*) among the rebels.

Compared with the highly organized Christian Union, which was reported to number 300,000 adherents, the origins of revolt often appear simple and uncontrived. The pattern of revolt was remarkably similar in many centres. It usually began with a handful of men in a village or town who had known one another for some time and discussed their wrongs at inns, bathhouses or other common meeting places (document VII). Rarely were they at first influenced by outside agitators or men of higher social status, and even direct incitement by lower clergy or lay preachers of strong Protestant leanings was infrequent (but see document VIII). Once the decision was taken to recruit more supporters, the circle of those in the know was widened on the snowball principle by individual conversations at markets, on pilgrimages, at the annual church ales celebrated by every parish church, and on other occasions when people congregated naturally without arousing suspicion. Leaders now had to be sought with the qualities necessary to further the interests of groups larger than a single village, and these tended to come from the ranks of rural or urban craftsmen, small traders, lesser clergy, ex-mercenaries, or officials of the lords, who might not themselves have grievances or be eager to lead a revolt (document VII). Once men assembled under arms, perhaps on a large heath or a hill-top, the transition took place from the community of the village, parish or court to the troop of soldiers gathering in a circle to make policy decisions by majority vote and to elect their own captains, standard bearers and sergeants. These peasant troops employed various means to secure compliance with their wishes. Letters sent from village to village threatened any who would not join with an attack on their persons and property (document IX). Whether out of sympathy for the cause or fear, few such invitations were refused, and refusal sometimes prompted implementation of the threats originally made (document VII). Nearly as common was what would today be called the boycott, enforced against individual villagers by driving a stake into the ground in front of their houses. The secular ban, as it was known, is best described in the letter of the Black Forest rebels, probably drafted by the Reformer Balthasar Hubmayer of Waldshut, which was sent to the towns of Freiburg and Villingen (document X). However, the sense of class solidarity among peasants which these and similar documents exhibited did not usually extend beyond the province in which they originated; nor did peasant unity and organization prove sufficient in the end to overcome the superior military resources and the greater degree of cooperation which prevailed among the members of the Swabian League and other German rulers.

I. *The Twelve Articles, 27 February—1 March 1525*[1]

The basic and correct chief articles of all the peasants and subjects of ecclesiastical and secular lords, concerning matters on which they feel themselves aggrieved.

To the Christian reader: Peace and the grace of God through Christ.

There are many Antichrists who have recently taken the assemblies of peasants as a pretext to pour scorn on the Gospel, saying 'Are these the fruits of the new Gospel, that no one should be obedient, but everywhere rise in revolt, assemble in great strength and conspire to reform and overthrow the ecclesiastical and secular authorities, perhaps even to kill them?' The following articles refute all these Godless and malicious critics, serving firstly to remove this calumny on the Word of God, and secondly to give a Christian response to the charge that all peasants are disobedient or indeed rebellious. In the first place the Gospel is not the cause of revolts or disorders, since it is a message about Christ, the promised Messiah, whose Word and life teach nothing but love, peace, patience and concord, so that all who believe in this Christ become loving, peaceful, patient and of one mind. Therefore the purpose of all the articles of the peasants (as will clearly be seen) is directed towards hearing the Gospel and living according to it. How then can the Antichrists call the Gospel a cause of revolt and disobedience? That some Antichrists and enemies of the Gospel resist these demands and requests is not due to the Gospel, but to the Devil, the most dangerous enemy of the Gospel, who by means of unbelief arouses such opposition among his followers. The Word of God (which teaches love, peace and concord) is thereby suppressed and taken away. Secondly, it follows clearly that the peasants who ask for this Gospel as their teaching and life may not be called disobedient or rebellious. Now if God intends to hear the peasants (who plead anxiously to be allowed to live according to His Word), who shall find fault with the will of God? Who shall meddle in His judgement? Who indeed shall oppose His majesty? Did He hear the children of Israel when they cried out to Him, and deliver them from the hand of Pharaoh? Can He not still save His own today? Yes, He will save them, and that speedily. Therefore, Christian reader, read the following articles with care, and then decide.

Here follow the articles:

THE FIRST ARTICLE

Firstly, we humbly ask and request—and it is the will and intention of us all—that in future we should have full authority for the whole community itself to elect and choose a pastor; and that we should also have the power to depose him should he conduct himself improperly. The same elected pastor should preach the Holy Gospel to us purely, clearly, and without the addition of human teaching and commandment. For to proclaim to us continually the true faith encourages us to ask God for His grace, that He may instil the same true faith into us and confirm it. For if the grace of God is not instilled in us, we remain always flesh and blood, which is worth nothing. As Scripture clearly says, we can come to God only through true faith, and can be saved only through His mercy. That is why we need such a leader and pastor; and thus our demand is grounded in Scripture.

THE SECOND ARTICLE

Secondly, although the true tithe is enjoined in the Old Testament but replaced in the New, nevertheless we will gladly pay the true corn tithe, but it must be done properly. Since one should give it to God and divide it among His servants, it belongs to a pastor who proclaims the word of God clearly. We intend that in future this tithe shall be collected and received by our churchwarden, whom the whole community appoints. From it he shall give to the priest who will be elected by the whole community a decent and sufficient sustenance for himself and his dependants, according to the judgement of the whole community. The remainder shall be distributed to the needy poor who happen to be present in the same village, according to circumstances and the judgement of the community. Any further remainder should be kept in case it becomes necessary to go to war for defence of the country; it should be paid for out of this surplus, so that no taxation may be imposed on the poor man. Should it be that one or more villages have sold the tithe themselves out of some necessity, the person who can prove to them purchase from the whole village is not to suffer loss. We shall instead come to a proper agreement with him according to the circumstances, to redeem the tithe from him in suitable instalments over a period of time. Should anyone not have bought the tithe from a village, but their forefathers have appropriated it for themselves, we will not, we should not, and we are no longer obliged to pay him any more, but only, as said above, to maintain our elected pastor with the tithe, and then to gather in the rest or, as is written in Holy Scripture, distribute it to the needy, whether they are clerical or lay. The small tithe we will not pay at all, for the Lord God created cattle for the free use of man, and we regard it as an improper tithe which men have invented; therefore we will not render it any longer.

THE THIRD ARTICLE

Third, it has until now been the custom for lords to assume that we are their serfs. This is detestable, seeing that Christ by the shedding of His precious blood has redeemed and bought us all, the shepherd equally with the highest, no one excepted. Therefore it is proven from

Scripture that we are free and wish to be free. Not that we wish to be completely free, to have no authority, for God does not teach us that. We should live according to the commandments, not the free licence of the flesh; but we are to love God, to recognize Him as our Lord in our neighbour, and to perform everything (as we gladly would do) which God commanded us at the Last Supper. Therefore we ought to live according to His commandment; this commandment does not direct and teach us not to obey authority, but rather that we should humble ourselves towards everyone, not just the rulers. Thus we willingly obey our chosen and appointed rulers (whom God has appointed over us) in all proper and Christian matters. And we have no doubt that, as true and genuine Christians, you will gladly release us from serfdom or show us in the Gospel that we are serfs.

THE FOURTH ARTICLE

Fourth, it has until now been the custom that no poor man has been permitted to catch game, wild fowl, or fish in flowing water, which seems to us quite improper and unbrotherly, and indeed selfish and not according to the Word of God. In some places the lords preserve the game to our distress and enormous loss. We must suffer that the unreasoning animals wantonly and to no purpose devour our crops (which God has caused to grow for man's use); it is ungodly and unneighbourly that we have to keep quiet about this practice. For when the Lord God created man, He gave him dominion over all animals, over the bird in the air and over the fish in the water. Therefore it is our request that if anyone has waters, he should prove with satisfactory documents that the waters have been intentionally sold to him. In that case we do not ask that they be taken from him by force; for the sake of brotherly love, one should rather show Christian consideration in the matter. But whoever cannot offer sufficient proof should surrender the waters to the community in a proper manner.

THE FIFTH ARTICLE

Fifth, we also have a grievance about cutting wood, for our lords have appropriated the woods to themselves alone, and when the poor man needs some wood, he must buy it at a double price. In our opinion the woods held by lords, whether ecclesiastical or secular, who have not bought them, should revert to the entire community. The community should be free to allow everyone, in an orderly manner, to use what he needs for firewood at home without charge, and also to take building timber without charge and when necessary, though with the knowledge of the official elected by the community for that purpose. If there are no woods except those which have been correctly purchased, a brotherly and Christian agreement should be reached with the owner; but if the property had first been arbitrarily expropriated and afterwards sold, agreement should be reached according to the facts of the case and the understanding of brotherly love and the Holy Scriptures.

THE SIXTH ARTICLE

Sixth is our grievous burden of labour services, which are increased from day to day in amount and variety. We ask that a proper investigation be made and that such heavy burdens be not laid upon us; let our case be graciously examined, according as our forefathers performed their services, but also according to the tenour of the Word of God.

THE SEVENTH ARTICLE

Seventh, in the future we shall not allow a lord to oppress us further. Rather, a man shall possess his holding according to the proper terms on which it has been leased, that is by the agreement between lord and peasant. The lord should not compel him further in any way, by asking for more services or other dues without recompense, so that the peasant may use and enjoy his property unburdened and in peace. But if the lord requires services, the peasant should willingly serve his own lord before others, but at a time and day not to the disadvantage of the peasant, and for suitable payment.

THE EIGHTH ARTICLE

Eighth, many of us who have farms are aggrieved that these cannot yield the rents, and the peasants lose their property thereby and are ruined. The lords should have honourable men inspect these farms and fix a fair rent, so that the peasant does not work for nothing; for every labourer is worthy of his hire.

THE NINTH ARTICLE

Ninth, we are aggrieved in matters of criminal jurisdiction, for which new laws are continually being made. Punishment is inflicted on us not according to the facts in the case, but at times by great ill-will, and at times by great partiality. In our opinion we should be punished with old written penalties, and according to the circumstances, not partiality.

THE TENTH ARTICLE

Tenth, we are aggrieved that some have expropriated meadows or arable fields that once belonged to a community. These we shall restore to communal ownership, unless they have been correctly purchased. If they have been improperly purchased, an amicable and brotherly agreement should be reached by the parties according to the facts of the case.

THE ELEVENTH ARTICLE

Eleventh, we wish to have the custom called heriot completely abolished. We shall never tolerate it nor allow widows and orphans to be so shamefully deprived and robbed of their property, contrary to God and honour, as has happened in many places and in various ways. They have flayed and scraped us from that property which they ought to guard and protect; if they had had the slightest legal claim, they would have taken it all. God will no longer suffer it; it shall be entirely done away with. Henceforth no man shall be obliged to pay anything, neither a small sum nor a large one.

CONCLUSION

Twelfth, it is our conclusion and final resolution that if one or more of the articles set forth here were not to be in agreement with the Word of God (though we think this is not so), these articles should be demonstrated to us to be inadmissable by the Word of God, and we would abandon them, when it is explained to us on the basis of Scripture. Should some of the articles be granted now and later be found unjust, they should be null and void from that hour, no more of any value. Likewise, if more articles shall be truthfully found in Scripture that are contrary to God and a burden on fellow men, we reserve these also and wish to have them included in our resolution. We will exercise and prove ourselves in all Christian doctrine, for which we shall pray to the Lord God; for He, and no one else, can give it to us. The peace of Christ be with us all.

II. *The Villages Oepfingen and Griesingen against Junker Ludwig von Freiberg, before 16 February 1525*[2]

The articles and grievances, which we of Oepfingen together with we of Griesingen have against the noble and honourable Junker Ludwig von Freiberg.

1. Item firstly, when it happens that military service is performed, the military contributions are imposed on us poor persons, but we claim not to owe this money for the reason that we pay rent and dues so that our Junker should properly protect and guard us.

2. Further, our Junker makes demands on us because of serfdom, but we claim not to be obliged to be serfs for the reason that we are burdened with marriage dues and also with heriots and death dues and others because of serfdom; when a poor man takes a wife who is not the lord's, he has to come to terms with the lord according to the latter's pleasure.

3. Further, our Junker demands of us such large, heavy, daily service, which we must perform without limit, that on no day do we know in the morning when we get up whether we are safe from serving him; no one could tolerate this burden of which we complain.

4. Further, when some of us poor people who farm for a one third share of the crop give the Junker the third, he gives them neither straw nor pig-food from this third, so that the poor man may not keep animals according to his need; meanwhile our Junker has all the more

animals, so that the community is harmed and overburdened; for these animals the villages must pay a shepherd appointed at the lord's pleasure.

5. Further, when it happens that a poor man has one meadow or more on which he pays an annual rent, our Junker has as large a stud farm as he wants, who daily pasture on such meadows as are prescribed; the village is harmed and overburdened so that we claim that we should be relieved from this grievance.

6. Further, when one of his poor subjects has a heap of manure, he goes there and takes it, giving the poor man nothing; they claim to be harmed and overburdened by this practice.

7. Further, a poor man who has neither house nor farm, but nothing except what he can earn with his work, finds that when this income is at its best he must work for his lord for several days without pay; this is a great loss and grievance to them, and they claim relief from both these articles.

8. Further, since the [elected] Four in a village have sworn to the bailiff to do the very best for the village, these Four should themselves issue bye-laws and regulations, and whenever their ordinances for the village are broken, the fines should belong to the village; nevertheless, our Junker's officials have seized these fines, which is harmful and burdensone to the community.

9. Further, should it happen that storms came or some other calamity, whether by fire or flood, whereby the common man loses his crops in field or barn, the poor man to whom this happens claims that, before he pays his rent, the landlord should lose his rent as well as the poor man his crop.

10. Further, the innkeeper at Oepfingen complains that his Junker leased him the tavern and promised that no other innkeeper would be admitted into his jurisdiction during the innkeeper's lifetime. But now the Junker has allowed another to sell wine. Thereupon the innkeeper who makes this complaint went to his Junker and asked him honestly to uphold what he had promised and give him the advantage. Until now the innkeeper has had no success. He claims that he has suffered damage and been overburdened; as long as there is another innkeeper, he should not owe his Junker any rent.

11. Further, our Junker has a mill to which he compels us, so that we must grind our corn there; the common man complains that this harms and overburdens him.

12. Further, hitherto whenever a poor man died, the lords raised the entry fines and rents on the farms and took away several pieces of arable and meadow from them, so that the poor man is harmed and overburdened.

13. Further, the village of Griesingen must give the bailiff thirty-five shillings every year, and we must allow him to pasture four head

of cattle without charge on our commons; the community claims this harms and overburdens it.

14. Further, some poor people at Griesingen hold farms of the abbot of Ochsenhausen which in living memory have never escheated without judicial process, but now the abbot of Ochsenhausen pretends that whenever someone dies on such farms [as are in arrears with rent], they should fall in to him without obstruction from any of the heirs. Now some time ago they lost their goods in a fire, and before that in storms and hail, so that the poor people could not pay these rents. But now the abbot of Ochsenhausen claims that the poor people should pay those rents now and in the future, which harms and overburdens the poor man.

15. Further, when we poor folk in good faith explained our need for improvements and for the assembly now taking place among the people, our Junker mistreated us for it and said that he would never forget our actions; if he died, other lords would come after him, and he trusted that they would also behave in this way. They therefore complain of the harm done by such enmity on the part of their Junker.

The matter cannot be left at that; several further articles have to be written down that are not yet sufficiently indicated nor yet revealed, articles with which the poor common man has been so severely harmed and overburdened, and still is, and in so many ways, that one cannot adequately talk about it. Item, several people have been forced out of their property which is their own and bought dearly and properly according to law, but which they neither can nor may enjoy or use according to their need; they have been imprisoned and put into the stocks for their possessions, for which God have mercy, and dared not speak the truth nor ask for justice, whereby we have become poor men. We are of the opinion that the poor man is also entitled to justice and the ruler should use no force. Item, it has however been the practice and still is, that when a poor man has asked for justice, the nobleman seized the poor man by the doublet and said: I will do you justice, and placed him in a prison. This the poor man had to suffer, when faithless injustice was done to him.

III. Articles compiled in the Allgäu, mid-February to mid-March, 1525[3]

1. Item that the parishes [should be filled] with sensible priests and none under forty years old to be taken.

2. No leave of absence from parishes to be given, but to be occupied in person.

3. The sacraments and holy rites should no longer be sold, but given to every Christian person for God's sake.

4. A child is no longer to be denied burial.

5. All who receive spiritual alms and do not keep to the priestly conduct laid down in their statutes should be deposed from their offices and pensions.

The Peasants of Swabia

6. No clergy should judge over capital crimes again.

7. All clergy should be subordinate to temporal judges in secular matters.

8. All clerics should pay tithe on their landed property to their princes and lords.

9. The clerics should be obliged as are laymen for territorial taxes and military contributions.

10. The clergy should not engage in secular commerce any more.

11. Payments for safe conduct should be abolished; every lord should preserve free passage through his land.

12. Death dues not to be given any longer.

13. To marry whom they wanted.

14. Freedom of movement [to live] under whichever [lord] they wanted.

15. To sell their own property freely, giving the lords nothing thereof.

16. Not to burden landed property with taxes above old custom.

17. [To leave them] with fines and punishments at the old level, as is the law in the *Tigen* of Rettenberg.[4]

18. All flowing waters should be free [for fishing].

19. Birds, chickens, hares and wild pigs should be free.

20. When a peasant dies, the lords should no longer share his inheritance with the children.

21. Wrecks of ships or carts on the roads should be abolished [as a lord's prerogative].

22. To pay no more excise or tolls on food.

23. No crops, wine, corn or others to be sold to the lords [under compulsion].

IV. *Complaints against the Abbot of Kempten by his subjects, 1524*[5]

1. Konrad Fraydinng [of the parish of Durach], serf, had a wife who died; he had to share her inheritance with the abbot and paid him 50 fl. [Rhenish gulden]. Then he took another wife, who was a free *Zinser*. She died on him also. But my lord again wanted half the inheritance. He had to give him 30 fl. Then he took a third wife, who died on him also. The abbot then took the half share again, and he had to pay him 20 fl. In the end he died himself. The half share was taken again. His children therefore found these monies paid out in advance. Nothing was left except 18 pounds *Heller*. The abbot wanted to have this sum as well. Then the children did not want to give him anything. He took everything and some of the children had to go begging. They would have been spared this fate, had their father's property not been taken away in this manner.

2. Hans Rych [of the parish of Untrasried] and Elss Schraglini his lawful wife, both free *Zinser*, were both arrested before they ever came together, about 4 years earlier, and each had to give a written promise not to leave the abbey's territories and not to take a wife or husband

without the abbot's permission. My lord of Kempten then took her to his castle as a maid, where she fell in love with the good Rych and he also with her; he pursued her so long until she took him in marriage, to which the hot blood of love had driven them both; they had no thought for the troublesome written undertaking they had made, and believed that no wrong had been done, since she is a free *Zinser*, and he also, and they remained within the lordship and had taken the sacrament of holy matrimony. For this he was captured and beaten and lay in prison 14 weeks less 2 days; if he wanted his release, he had to pay 565 fl. and above that secure guarantors for 700 fl., swear a grievous oath, and make a written promise never to reopen the matter at law or outside the law, neither before popes nor before emperors or kings. The authority and power of royal majesty and papal power are thereby shut out, as we free *Zinser* all complain; for Rych himself is a free *Zinser*, and his wife too, and until today they still live by the law and custom of *Zinser*.

3. Peter Owl of Geschwend in the parish of St. Peter's valley, a free *Zinser*, has an allod farm. He complains of the prelates of the abbey of Kempten that at times when severe drought had come upon the corn or hail had flattened it, he had often asked the ruling prelates of the abbey to allow him to sell an annuity of money or corn, so that he and his children should not go hungry and be robbed of the means of feeding themselves. The prelates never wanted to allow him to sell an annuity except to subjects of the abbey, but his farm lies within the sovereignty of the bishop of Augsburg, so that he may only find purchasers who are subjects of the bishop but not of the abbey, since his farm is too far away for the latter. He asks that in future, for the sake of his children's sustenance, an annuity should be raised on his farm when similar occasions arise, so that he and his family should not go hungry and suffer harm to their persons, as happened when he had had to sell the cattle and horses by means of which he had fed himself and his children.

V. *Ordinance for the League of Allgäu Peasants, 7 March 1525*[6]

Actions and articles resolved, on the Monday after Invocavit, by all companies of the peasant troops who allied together in the name of the holy undivided Trinity.

For the praise and honour of the almighty everlasting God and the exaltation of the Holy Gospel and God's Word, the Christian Union and alliance has been established to aid the cause of justice and divine law, without prejudice or disadvantage to anyone, whether he is clerical or lay, according as the Gospel and divine law teach, and especially to increase brotherly love.

1. Firstly, the honourable assembly of this Christian Union offers not to oppose in any way the obligations due according to divine law to ecclesiastical or temporal rulers, but to remain obedient.

2. It is the intention and opinion of the honourable assembly, that the common peace be kept in the province and no one do another injustice. If it should happen that someone should be moved to war and disturbance against another, no one should assemble or take sides in any way, and the neighbours, of whatever estate, should have power to make and command peace. Peace should be observed immediately when it is first enjoined or proclaimed, and whoever will not keep it shall be punished according to his offence.

3. Admitted arrears of debts, or those for which there are sealed letters or authentic rent-rolls, shall be paid. But if someone should claim to have an objection, he shall be entitled to legal recourse, but each at his own expense, without involving the common assembly of this Christian Union. Future debts, like tithes and other rents and dues, shall be suspended until the issues are settled.

4. If there are castles situated in this province and not allied with this Christian Union, the owners of these castles shall be required by a friendly warning not to supply their castles further than with provisions for their proper sustenance, and not to garrison these castles either with cannon or with persons who have not joined this alliance. If however they increase the garrison beyond previous strength, they shall do so with people who are allied to and members of this alliance, at their own cost and expense; similarly the monasteries.

5. Servants who serve princes and lords shall renounce their oaths and be admitted to this alliance when they do so; whoever refuses to do it shall take wife and children and leave the province unmolested. If a lord summons an official or another member of this alliance, he should not go alone, but take two or three others with him and let them hear what is said to him.

6. Priests or vicars shall be required and asked in a friendly manner to proclaim and preach the Holy Gospel. The parish should give seemly maintenance to any cleric who would do this. Whichever of them would not do so shall be dismissed, and the parish provided with another.

7. If someone should wish to enter into an agreement with his superior lord, he shall not conclude it without the previous knowledge and consent of the common assembly of this alliance. And if the agreement is concluded with the consent of the said assembly, the persons concerned should nevertheless consent to the perpetual alliance and Christian Union, and remain within it.

8. Each troop of this alliance shall appoint and send a commander and four councillors; they shall have the authority to act together with the other commanders and councillors, as is proper, so that the whole community need not always come together.

9. No stolen goods purloined from these members shall be kept or change hands.

10. Any craftsman who wishes to leave the province in order to follow his trade should swear to the captain of his parish not to allow

himself to be recruited against this Christian Union, but if he should hear that something hostile is intended against this assembly, he shall inform this alliance of it and, if it becomes necessary, immediately return to his fatherland and help to save it. Soldiers should be placed under a similar obligation.

11. The courts and justice shall take their course as before.

12. Improper games, blasphemy and drinking competitions are forbidden. Whoever does not observe this shall be punished according to his offence.

VI. Articles of the Oath of the Christian Union, early March 1525[7]

The articles we have sworn to one another.

Item that we want men of skill and understanding in Holy Scripture to preach and teach us the Holy Gospel and the Word of God purely, clearly, and without the addition of human teaching and its fruits.

Secondly, that we will offer and submit to divine and Christian justice, against anyone who has hitherto oppressed us, in the appropriate places, if they also accept it.

Thirdly, that we have not sworn together against God or anyone else, except whoever will not let us carry out our intentions, and that no one shall swear against his lord and ruler or oppose him further than is contained in the above articles.

VII. The Beginnings of Revolt in Upper Swabia: The Chronicle of Johannes Kessler of St. Gallen[8]

When the hour was at hand, at which the fire of this revolt was to be lit, it happened in Shrovetide (as it is called), when people are accustomed to visit one another, that about six or seven peasants in a village near Ulm, called Baltringen, came together and discussed many of the current troubles. As was the custom among peasants at that time, they travelled from one village to another as if calling on neighbours, and ate and drank together in convivial fashion; the peasants in the village then also journeyed onwards with them. If anyone asked where they were going or what they were doing, they replied, 'We are fetching Shrovetide cakes from one another'. And in such company they travelled about every Thursday and grew every time in numbers, until they were four hundred men.

Now on the eighth day before Shrove Tuesday, which was the 26th day of February [the dating is wrong], they assembled again at Baltringen; and when they saw the crowd before their eyes, and how they had so multiplied, they said to one another, 'We have become many, and should this our assembly come to the notice of the lords, they might think ill of us for it and not take it in the spirit in which we intend it. Therefore let us consider how we should conduct ourselves'.

When they were all sitting together in assembly, they again considered their grievances, each complaining to the other of where the shoe pinched most. Finally they discussed the means by which they might achieve a reduction of their burdens, and decided first to complain strongly about their oppression to their lords and superiors, and then to ask for mercy and a reduction in their obligations. But when they looked around, they found no one in their midst who had ever been accustomed to speak before lords or who knew how to broach the matter properly.

On making serious enquiries, they were told that a pious, goodhearted and wise man, experienced in speaking, lived in the village of Sulmingen, Ulrich Schmid by name and trade. They resolved to ask him to take up their cause as leader and to conduct their affairs. Then they went to Sulmingen to explain their intentions to the said Ulrich Schmid. Thereupon they begged him most earnestly to become their leader, since there was no one among them who had ever been accustomed to have dealings with lords in any way.

When Ulrich learned their purpose, he did not immediately wish to comply or give them his consent, until he was overcome after many and various requests, and because he saw that in part their aims were not entirely unjust. But before he would give his consent, he wanted it expressly stated as a condition that everyone should know that he had no intention of bringing any complaints at all against his own lords concerning himself and his obligations. Because he was skilled in a good trade and had adequate sustenance for himself, his wife and children, he asked for nothing more and had no claims at all against any of his lords. But what he now nevertheless undertook to do, was done by him as a mediator, as a go-between for their and their lords' affairs, and his action should not be understood otherwise.

VIII. The Confession of Simon Lochmeir, ca. October 1525[9]

[Unusual features of this confession are the close connection between the heretical beliefs of a lay preacher and his incitement to rebellion and, for Swabia, the desire for no lord but the Emperor. The admission that the peasants wanted to kill all their enemies was probably forced on Lochmeir by his interrogators.]

Subjects of the widow of the late Hans von Freiberg.

Simon Lochmeir confesses firstly that he was the first author and plotter who roused and started the so-called Winzer troop [north-east of Memmingen, near Kulmbach], and that at Raunau at the very beginning he also incited to rebellion Paul Finden, Hans Bisseler, and Veit Lutzenberger, and decided with them to begin preaching the Lutheran sect from a cart at Rohr. At the third and fourth sermons he assembled as many as seven thousand people and proclaimed to them that everyone should be free and have no lord except the Emperor alone. He gave so many of these sermons that he does not know the number, and was also supreme captain of the same troop for a week, and thereafter a member of its council throughout; whatever blood was shed by that troop, he had taken part.

He confesses further that when the peasants at Merschweiler had been obedient to their superiors and had not wanted to join their league or brotherhood, he helped to take twelve horses from them by night without due legal summons or declaration of a feud; [from the sale of these horses] they obtained their communal provisions, and he received in addition one and a half gulden, less three kreutzer, from the surplus.

He confesses further that he helped to plunder the monastery of Roggenburg [24 June] and Conz von Rietheim's castle of Hohenraunau [May], and told another he should set Unterraunau alight; he also received one gulden as his share of Conz von Rietheim's ransom.

He confesses further that he urged the troop to kill, destroy, burn out and devastate all those who were in the Swabian League and whoever opposed their brotherhood.

He confesses again that at Hohenraunau he helped to take a cart of coarse flax.

He confesses further that he was their leader; at the beginning he made all the inhabitants in the above-named places abandon their loyalty to nobles, cities and monasteries, brought them to his allegiance, and resolved with them that none of them would any longer obey or give service to any lord.

He confesses moreover that he also had a great liking for the Lutheran sect and misled many people with him and made them disobedient.

He confesses also that for him neither the mother of God nor the beloved saints may intercede with God nor mediate with Him in any way. He had also allowed two daughters to die without confession or the holy sacrament, since he has no belief in those articles, but they are signs and God is in the Word.

IX. Summons of the Brandenburg Troop to Villagers in Franconia, 2 May 1525[10]

From the elected captains of the troop in the margraviate [of Ansbach].

Greetings. Dear brethren in Christ, we command you in earnest that you come to us straightly and without delay to the city of Dinkelsbühl to proclaim the Holy Gospel, of which many of our brethren have been robbed by force, and to relieve certain burdens which we, they, and you cannot bear. If you do not, we shall visit you in a way that will not please you at all, and we shall attack your persons. Know therefore how you must act. If you do not comply within two days of being shown this letter, what is written in it will be performed. Given at Gerbertshofen.

X. Circular Letter of the Black Forest Peasants, before 8 May 1525[11]

Honourable, wise and kind lords, friends and dear neighbours. Until now great oppressions, contrary to God and all justice, have been imposed on the poor common man in towns and in the countryside by ecclesiastical and lay lords and rulers, whom they have however not touched with the smallest finger. It follows therefore that such burdens and oppressions cannot be borne or tolerated any longer, unless the common poor man wants to drive himself and his descendants into complete beggary. Therefore it is the plan and intention of this Christian Union to make themselves free with the aid of God, and to do it as far as is possible without drawing sword and shedding blood; this cannot indeed be done without brotherly urging and an alliance in all seemly matters affecting the Christian commonweal, as set out in the following articles. It is our friendly request, desire and brotherly entreaty that you willingly enter with us into this Christian Union and brotherhood, and do so in a friendly spirit, so that the Christian commonweal and brotherly love again become established, built up and increased. If you do this, God's will shall be done in fulfilment of his command of brotherly affection. But if you refuse this request, which we do not expect at all, we pronounce you in the secular ban and declare you to be under the ban by virtue of this letter, until such time as you abandon your purpose and yield yourselves up in a favourable spirit to this Christian Union. In good faith we did not wish to conceal this from you as our dear lords, friends and neighbours. We therefore ask for a written answer from your council and common assembly by the same messenger. Herewith may you be commended to God.

The secular ban has this form: all who are in this Christian alliance, bound by honour and the high oaths they have made, shall keep no community at all with those who oppose and resist entering the brotherly alliance and will not further the Christian commonweal. There shall be no community of eating, drinking, bathing, milling, baking, ploughing or mowing with them, nor shall food, corn, drink, timber, meat, salt and other provisions be delivered to them, nor shall anyone else be allowed to make such delivery, nor should one buy anything from them or sell to them, but let them remain cut off in these respects as dead members who do not wish to further, but rather to hinder, the Christian commonweal and the peace of the province. All markets, woods, commons, pasture and waters which do not lie within their boundaries shall be barred to them. Whoever of those who have entered this alliance overlooks these rules shall also be excluded in the future and be punished with the same ban and sent out with wife and children to our opponents and enemies.

Of castles, monasteries and ecclesiastical foundations: since all forms of damage, danger and ruin have come upon us from castles, monasteries and ecclesiastical foundations, they shall immediately be proclaimed in the ban. If however nobles, monks or clerics willingly wish to leave such castles, monasteries or foundations and to enter ordinary houses, like other people, and to join this Christian Union, they shall be received in friendly and seemly manner together with their property and possessions. Thereafter everything which is their due and belongs to them according to divine law shall be faithfully and honourably rendered to them without any objection.

Of those who house, support and maintain the enemies of this Christian Union: all those who house, support and maintain the enemies of this Christian Union shall be asked in a similar friendly manner to desist. But if they do not do so, they shall also be immediately pronounced in the secular ban.

NOTES

1. The original German in Franz [1963: 174-9]. Previous translations sometimes sacrificed accuracy to obtain a modern English idiom. This new version has benefited most from that in *Luther's Works* [1967: vol. 46, 8-16].
2. Translated from Franz [1963: 156-9].
3. Translated from Franz [1963: 163-5].
4. A league of some 12,000 taxpayers subject to the bishop of Augsburg; the surmise by F. Roth that they were responsible for all these articles remains unproven.
5. Translated from Franz [1963: 125]; Allgemeines Staatsarchiv, Munich, Fürststift Kempten, Münchener Bestand, Lit. 217, fos. 249R, 282R.
6. Translated from Franz [1963: 195-7].
7. Translated from Franz [1963: 197-8].
8. Translated from Franz [1963: 143-4]. Kessler's *Sabbata* was based on reports by participants in the revolt.
9. Allgemeines Staatsarchiv, Munich, Kriegsakten 75, fos. 298R-9R.
10. Translated from Bensen [1840: 388].
11. Translated from Franz [1963: 235-6].

REFERENCES

Bensen, Heinrich W., 1840, *Geschichte des Bauernkrieges in Ostfranken*, Erlangen.
Blickle, Peter, 1973, *Landschaften im Alten Reich*, Munich.
Buszello, Horst, 1969, *Der deutsche Bauernkrieg von 1525 als politische Bewegung*, Berlin.
Franz, Günther, 1936, 'Die Entstehung der "Zwölf Artikel" der deutschen Bauernschaft', *Archiv für Reformationsgeschichte*, XXXVI, 193-213.
Franz, Günther, ed., 1963, *Quellen zur Geschichte des Bauernkrieges*, Darmstadt.
Franz, Günther, 9th ed., 1969, *Der deutsche Bauernkrieg*, Darmstadt.
Guerrini, Paolo, 1947, 'I postulati della riforma nell'alta Italia', *Rivista di Storia della Chiesa in Italia*, I, 292-3.
Luther, M., 1967, *Luther's Works*, Philadelphia.
Roth, Friedrich, 1896, *Die Chroniken der deutschen Städte vom 14. bis ins 16. Jahrhundert*, 25, *Augsburg*, vol. 5, Leipzig.
Sabean, David, 1972, *Landbesitz und Gesellschaft am Vorabend des Bauernkrieges*, Stuttgart.
Sanuto, Marino, 1893, *I Diarii*, ed. F. Stefani et al., Venice.

Images of the Peasant, 1514–1525

R. W. Scribner*

The following illustrations and commentary examine some of the visual images of the peasant found in popular literature and propaganda at the time of the German Peasant War. The historian of such popular movements is often preoccupied with written source materials, understandable enough in the context of the early sixteenth century. The development of printing and the spread of literacy represent a major social and cultural phenomenon, and the waves of written polemic and propaganda which flooded Germany as the great debate on religion unwound during 1520-25 created the first genuine mass literature and mass audience of the modern period. It is all too easy, therefore, to overlook visual evidence, but we argue two reasons why it is so important.

Late-medieval popular culture was intensely visual, expressing itself in pageants, festivals, carnival plays and religious drama. An understanding of popular and peasant mentalities, rich in visual connotations, allusions and symbols, can be gleaned from the sifting of pictorial evidence, especially where this is reflected only incompletely or obliquely in written evidence. Secondly, stress on the importance of the printed word tells only half the story. Marshall McLuhan has emphasised that the invention of printing involved an enormous extension of man's visual sense [McLuhan, 1964 : 84], but this did not occur through the printed word alone. The development of printing occurred alongside and in conjunction with the development of mass pictorial reproduction, i.e. the print [Hind, 1963 : CLS. 3-5].

Where the printed word enabled communication through the exactly repeatable literary statement, the print made it possible through the exactly repeatable visual statement. If printing created a new source of information for the literate, the print fulfilled the same function for the illiterate and semi-literate, creating a tradition of communication carried on by cartoons, comic strips, newsreels and television [Ivins, 1969 : 2-4]. In a culture so strongly visual (witness the passions aroused during the Reformation by the matter of images of the saints!) the most effective early form of mass literature was predominantly visual: blockbooks, the *Bilderbogen* or primitive comic strip, and the broadsheet. As printing attained in Reformation literature the peak of its early influence, the woodcut, the cheapest and

*Lecturer in History, Portsmouth Polytechnic

most durable form of pictorial representation, reached the highpoint of its artistic development. It was used extensively in the titlepages and illustrations of printed pamphlets, and accompanied by a minimum of text formed the basis of the popular broadsheet. It became an integral part of Reformation propaganda, presenting pictorial images which drew on deep-rooted layers of popular consciousness. Above all it used its power of suggestion to create new associations of ideas and beliefs, which reinforced the impact of printed and spoken polemic.

The examples of the popular woodcut chosen for commentary present two aspects of the peasant image during the decade before the Peasant War. Firstly, the Reformation brought new ways of looking at the peasant, which were to influence the social evaluation and self-esteem of the peasantry. Secondly, it made explicit elements of popular belief which gave rise to hopes of fundamental changes in religion, state and society. Coalescing with a long tradition of peasant radicalism embodied in the *Bundschuh* movements, these found active expression in the rebellion of 1524-5.

One of the most important products of early Reformation propaganda was the figure of the Evangelical Peasant. Drawing on Luther's *theologia pauperum* and on pre-Reformation mysticism and primitivism, it embodied the notion that the common man stood closer to God than the priest, theologian or scholar [Uhrig, 1936: 95-106]. This involved an important shift in the social evaluation of the peasant, regarded previously as the lowest and most despised order of society. The peasant was classed among the most inferior occupations (the impoverished artisan, the gravedigger, the hangman and the mercenary) and associated with the dishonourable (beggars, vagrants and criminals). His stock literary image corresponded to this, presenting him as coarse, comic and stupid [ibid.: 77-94]. Even folk heroes such as the peasant Markolf, or Till Eulenspiegel, popular symbols of peasant cunning and raw rustic wit, were tainted with these lowly associations [Radbruch, 1961: 3-9, 26, 53].

The religious propaganda of the years 1520-25 reversed this low evaluation by creating a new positive image of the peasant as the chief supporter of the evangelical movement. The Evangelical Peasant was self-confident, wise and pious, speaking the truth in simple and pointed manner against the obscuring of it by priest and papist. He was a practical theologian, literate and knowledgeable in the Scripture, and he could dispute with, refute, even convert the opponents of the Gospel. He appeared as the author of tracts, even as a preacher [Uhrig, 1936]. The personification of this image was Karsthans, the peasant with the two-pronged hoe, the *Karst*, who appeared as early as 1520 as a presiding guardian over the emergence of the Gospel [Clemen, 1910: 1-133].

By identifying the fate of true religion with that of the 'common man' his social dignity was immeasurably increased, and the associated contempt for the religious and social role of the priest and the monk amounted to a complete inversion of traditional social values, which now placed the peasant in the forefront of hopes for the reform of religion and society. The power of this new image is seen in the figure of the Peasant of Wöhrd, a real-life manifestation of the fictional Karsthans. At the beginning of 1524 a preacher appeared in the village of Wöhrd near Nuremberg who attracted enormous crowds. Ostensibly a peasant who could neither read nor write, he revealed a good knowledge of Scripture, the Church Fathers and even the scholastic theologians. He had more than a passing acquaintanceship with Latin, Greek and Hebrew, and he was hailed as a wonder, a coarse and simple peasant inspired by the Holy Spirit. Even scholars spoke admiringly of him. In the course of time he was revealed as a fraud, a fugitive monk called Diepolt Beringer, and forbidden to preach by the authorities. Such however was the attraction of this 'Evangelical Peasant' that one of his sermons published in 1524 ran to no less than nine editions within a year [Clemen, 1902].

The importance of such images in creating widespread support for the Gospel was clearly perceived by the most skilful Catholic propagandist of the time, the Strassburg Franciscan, Thomas Murner. In his richly illustrated tract of 1522, *On the Great Lutheran Fool*, Murner tried to exploit these associations by linking the new movement to the threat of a peasant revolt. He depicted Luther in armour, greasing a *Bundschuh*, the leather peasant boot which had served as the symbol of peasant rebellion since 1502. Murner further tried to identify the allies of the Gospel with the feared German mercenaries, the *Landsknechte* [Merker, 1918]. His social perception was nicely calculated. Not only was the peasant associated with the foot-soldier in the contemporary image of the 'common man', but there was also a strong social connection between the two. The *Landsknechte* were mostly recruited from the rural classes and retained their sense of social identity by often refusing to fight against the peasants, whom they regarded as their brothers. Although the figure of the Evangelical Peasant was essentially peaceful, there was an ambivalence about it which Murner was quick to seize upon. The Evangelical Peasant was no merely passive supporter of the Gospel; if required he would spring to its defence in deed as well as word. Murner further saw that the identification of the fate of the Reformation with the 'common man' would encourage the peasants to press social demands which they felt were justified by Scripture itself.

Murner's sole misconception was to see the evangelical movement as simply providing an excuse for rebellion. However the propaganda of the early 1520s had stirred up deeper levels of popular religious consciousness. Throughout the fifteenth and early sixteenth centuries resentment at social and religious injustice had flowed easily into a broad stream of millenarian feeling which saw such abuses as evidence that the old corrupt world was in its death throes. These were signs presaging the coming of the Last Days, or at least of a new and more purified stage of mankind's journey towards salvation. This was confirmed in the immensely popular prophetic writings attributed to the twelfth-century abbot, Joachim of Flora, which told of the signs of a 'new age of the spirit'. At the end of the fifteenth century these Joachist ideas were further fostered by popular belief in astrology and its ability to predict the future. Since the 1480s there had appeared a growing number of prophecies foretelling fundamental changes in the human condition within the next generation. Their influence was accentuated by the eschatological tone of much of the Reformation propaganda. The ill-defined sense of foreboding to which this gave rise crystallised in part around the astrological belief that the conjunction of the planets would bring catastrophic effects onto mankind. This belief soon concentrated on the year 1524, when no less than 20 planetary conjunctions were expected, 16 of them in the sign of the fish. From this the astrologers deduced that a great deluge was to be awaited in February 1524, a prediction which provoked widespread fear and apprehension. In 1523 no less than 51 different prognostics appeared dealing with the flood, and a further 16 at the beginning of 1524. The sense of complete crisis was completed by predictions for that same year of a peasant rebellion [Strauss, 1926 : 69-70].

The defeat of the peasant rebellion of 1524-5 had a further radical effect on the image of the peasant. The ambivalence of the Karsthans figure was resolved in Murner's terms, and the peasant was seen as a figure of aggression. Luther dissociated himself and the evangelical movement from the peasant cause, and it was no longer an advantage to identify the Reformation with the 'common man'. The Evangelical Peasant virtually disappears from the popular literature of the Reformation after 1525 [Uhrig, 1936 : 190-93]. Certainly he was not replaced by any consistently hostile image, and the peasant was not presented again as a figure of fun or caricature. The high estimate of his social dignity of the early 1520s was succeeded by a mere curiosity about his life and culture. Artists sought to depict this in village fairs and festivals, but the essential sympathy of the earlier period is lacking [Radbruch, 1961 : 84-5]. Subsequently the Reformation itself came to regard popular culture as pagan and superstitious, and embarked on concerted attempts to 'reform' it. (The 'reformation of popular culture' during the latter part of the sixteenth and the seventeenth centuries has been described in a recent seminar paper by Peter Burke.)

Illustration 1

This depicts an early adaptation of the Karsthans theme in the titlepage of a Swiss pamphlet of 1521. Known as the 'Divine Mill', the picture invokes a tradition of pious representation of the doctrine of the Eucharist, seen in the illustrations *The Host Mill* and *Christ in the Wine Press*. (These show Christ the crucified Saviour being fed into a flourmill or winepress, from which emerge respectively the host and the wine of the Eucharist.) Here Christ shakes the grain of the Word—represented by St. Paul (with the sword) and the symbols of the four Evangelists (the lion, bull, eagle and the man) into the mill, where the production of the flour is supervised by Erasmus. This is a reference to Erasmus' 1516 edition of the New Testament, which was seen as reviving interest in biblical theology. The flour emerges as Faith, Hope, Charity and the Church, to be gathered into the floursack under the protection of the dove of the Holy Spirit. The symbol on the sack is possibly a millwheel surmounted by a cross. Just as a miller was identified by the sign on his sacks, so one can recognize the produce of the divine mill as that made from the fructifying grain of divine wisdom [Hegg, 1954].

Behind Erasmus, Luther is shown both baking this flour into the bread of the Bible, and attempting to distribute it. The pope, a cardinal, a bishop and a monk reject it, while a diabolical bird-dragon above them screeches 'Bann! Bann!' a reference to the papal condemnation of Luther. Behind Luther is Karsthans, his hoe replaced by a flail, which he wields in defence of the Gospel. No longer a symbol of passive piety or a mere disputant, Karsthans is shown acting positively in support of the evangelical message. From the heavens Christ as Lord of the World, identified by his cruciform halo, watches the scene, adding a note of eschatological urgency to the confrontation occurring below.

Dyss hand zwen schwytzer puren gmacht . . ., 1521, *Augsburg: Melchoir Ramminger.*
British Library 11517. *c.*58

Illustration 2 and 3

Although originally depicted with the *Karst*, Karsthans was more often given the flail as his attribute, and the peasant with the flail became the symbol of popular support for the Gospel. Thomas Murner's attempt to counteract this image involved depicting the allies of the Gospel as mercenary footsoldiers. In three illustrations he represented them as haughty *Landsknechte* bearing banners emblazoned 'Gospel', 'Freedom' and 'Truth'. The second of these (Illustration 2) is often incorrectly used as a depiction of

T. *Murner*, Von dem grossen Lutherischen Narr, 1522, *Strassburg*.
I. *Grienninger*, British Library 11517, c. 33.

Images of the Peasant

an insurgent peasant, but Murner intended it as a scornful derision of evangelical freedom, labelling it as the freedom of the brigand. That the illustrations were also intended to ridicule peasant support for the Gospel, and to reaffirm the charge that it would lead to rebellion, is shown in three other woodcuts in the same work. These show *Landsknechte* riding on a boar, a slug and a goose, each bearing a shield with a *Bundschuh*. Their weapons further identify them as peasants, the first and second carrying respectively a pitchfork and a rake. The second of these is reproduced as Illustration 3.

Illustration 4

One can see how clearly Murner's depiction of the insurgent peasant was a spiteful caricature if one examines this title page from a 1514 pamphlet on the *Bundschuh*, written by Pamphilus Gengenbach, a publisher and later Reformation polemicist from Basel. The peasant is clad in rural dress, wearing the protective headgear used for winter work in the fields. In the crook of his arm he holds the *Bundschuh* banner, while his left hand is clenched in the secret sign used by the insurgents, with the thumb held inside the folded fingers. He holds his sword, which peasants were not normally allowed to wear, in a defiant horizontal position, ready to be drawn if necessary.

The peasant banner recalls once again Murner's shrewd perception in using the 'Freedom Banner' to link the peasant to the mercenary. The insurgent peasants were indebted to the *Landsknechte* for certain features of their organization, especially for the use of flags as visual slogans and emotive rallying points. The flag had been used as an integral part of peasant rebellion since 1502 by the master organizer of the *Bundschuh* risings, Joss Fritz. Its importance is shown by the fact that Fritz delayed the risings in two and possibly three instances waiting for the completion of the banner, so risking the discovery of the conspiracy [*Radbruch, 1961 : 67-70; Steinmann, 1960 : 241, 266-7, 274*].

The banner itself is triangular. In the centre is the crucified Christ, flanked by Mary and John the Baptist, the two patrons chosen by the rebels as their protective saints. These, or rather their names, may also have served as a rallying cry in the heat of battle [*Steinmann, 1960 : 277*]. At the foot of the cross kneels a peasant, obscured by the head of the peasant holding the banner. The coats of arms to the left and right of this group were those of the emperor and the pope, a reference to the peasants' claim that they would recognize no lords other than these. Originally the blank coat of arms to the left bore an imperial eagle, surmounted by a crown. The publisher clearly found this explicit reference to the peasant programme to be politically embarrassing, and had the imperial eagle cut away from the block, although traces of it remain. For the same reason the papal tiara has been cut away above the coat of arms on the right. The heraldic emblem on the arms has been retained, presumably because it was less well-known in Germany. It is however that of the family of Pope Julius II (1503-13), a golden oak branch with three acorns on a blue field. (Although Julius II had died and been succeeded by Leo X some six months before the production of the flag, the peasants seem to have overlooked the fact.) The reverse side of the banner bore a *Bundschuh*, and since it was impossible to illustrate this in the woodcut, the artist has placed a *Bundschuh* on the ground beside the peasant. Finally, the plaque to the right of the peasant bears the date 1514, in mirror image. This indicates that the woodcut is possibly a copy of an earlier woodcut, but reversed left to right [*Steinmann, 1960 : 261-7*].

Der Bundtschu
Diß biechlein sagt von dem bö
sen fürnemen der Bundtschuher/ wye es sich
angefengt geendet vnd aus kumen ist.

¶ Pamphilus Gengenbach   R G F
Nyt me yegundt ist mein beger.
Ob yenen ainer vom bundtschu wer
Dem da für kem dieß schlecht gedicht
Bit ich er wels verachten nicht
So kumpt er nit yn solche not
Als mancher yetz ist bliben todt
Vngehorsam gou vngestrofft nit lot

P. Gengenbach, Der Bundschu. Diss biechlein sagt von dem bd . . ., 1514 *Augsburg: Erhard Öglin. Reproduced from Engels* [1956: 83].

Illustration 5

This is taken from an earlier edition of Gengenbach's work on the *Bundschuh*. It shows armed peasants swearing an oath of confederacy on the *Bundschuh* banner, with two index fingers and thumb upraised in the characteristic gesture of the time for oathtaking. The peasants, slightly ragged in dress, are armed with a mixture of swords, daggers and worktools—axes and a rake. The banner is a wholly incorrect rendition of the *Bundschuh* flag, resting no doubt on incorrectly reported facts. It is square rather than triangular, and the central group portrays Christ, Mary and John the Evangelist, instead of John the Baptist. A *Bundschuh* has been placed at the foot of the crucifix, and the kneeling peasant on the left is balanced by a kneeling woman on the right, possibly in imitation of religious paintings, where the donors are portrayed at the foot of the saints [Steinmann, 1961 : 259-61].

The depiction in the background constitutes a warning to the peasants. It represents the sacrifice of Isaac by Abraham, whom Gengenbach identifies in his pamphlet as a type of obedience to authority. Abraham, who wields the sword, may be dressed as an executioner, and so also represents secular authority, carrying out reluctantly the commands of the Lord. The angel staying Abraham's arm identifies the scene as a promise of mercy if the peasants are obedient. This is confirmed by the peasants busily tilling the fields nearby, a contrast to the rebellious peasants in the foreground, who are about to use their tools as weapons. The illustration reflects the tone of sympathetic condemnation adopted by Gengenbach in his pamphlet.

Images of the Peasant

P. Gengenbach, Der bundtschu. Diss biechlin sagt von dem bosen furnemen der Bundtschuher..., 1514, Basel: Gengenbach. British Library 11515.b.25. Reproduced from a copy kindly supplied by Dietz Verlag, Berlin.

Illustration 6

By contrast with Murner's polemic, the *Bundschuh* illustrations reveal the strong sense of social identity inherent in the peasant rebellions, and how effectively they had used elements drawn from both popular religion and the mercenary tradition without losing sight of their central purpose. This purposefulness and sense of identity characterises much of the propaganda for the Peasant War itself. Illustration 6 shows the title page of a peasant pamphlet of 1525, the *Memminger Bundesordnung,* which contained articles complementary to the Twelve Articles and rules of conduct for the peasants. This programme was the outcome of consultation in Memmingen (March 6-7 1525), where some 50 leaders of the three major troops of peasants in the Swabian area hammered out a compromise between different strategies. While some wished to adopt a radical and militant stance, others insisted on reform in the spirit of 'divine justice'. Later, on March 15, a list of mediators, including Luther, Melanchthon and Frederick the Wise, was added to the *Bundesordnung*. These were to negotiate with the Swabian League opposing the peasants, and although neither was accepted by the authorities, the pamphlet indicates the first success of a coordinated action among different centres of rebellion.

The woodcut depicts a peasant band clad in simple armour, a contrast to the often elaborate costume of the mercenaries. Some peasant leaders did adopt the more colourful dress of the *Landsknechte* [*Radbruch, 1961 : Ill. 39*], a reflection perhaps of the rôle played by some mercenaries who acted as peasant troop leaders. But for the most part the peasants' dress was simpler—work clothes or plain armour. Like the *Bundschuh* rebels, this band is armed with makeshift weapons (a pitchfork, flail and club), as well as the more usual halberd and spear. It mirrors the ambivalence of Karsthans himself: peaceful in intent, it will fight to uphold its cause. The peasant banner bears a ploughshare, a symbol of the just intention of the rising and of its defensive nature.

Handlung, Artickel, unnd Instruction, so fürgenommen worden sein vonn allen Rottenn unnd hauffen der Pauren . . ., 1525, *Augsburg: H. Steiner. British Library 9365.a.16.*

Illustration 7

This title page from a 1523 prognostic of Leonhart Reynmann takes as its central theme the prediction of the Great Flood expected in February 1524. It shows the conjunction of several planets in the sign of the Fish, producing a deluge which sweeps away a town and its inhabitants. The planets are identified by their astrological symbols as Saturn, Jupiter, Mars, Venus, Mercury, the Sun and the Moon. The figures grouped to the left and right of the flood represent Saturn and Jupiter as the major opposing forces. The astrologers regarded these as the two 'superior planets', which because of their slower orbits came only rarely into conjunction, indeed in the same sign only once about every 960 years. This was regarded as a 'Great Conjunction', producing particularly radical effects. Saturn was said to bring great misfortune for the state, and for the church as well, when in conjunction with Jupiter, which was held to rule over religion [*Strauss, 1926*: 67-8]. The conjunction of February 1524 was to be such a 'Great Conjunction', bringing death over the land (this appears to be the significance of the corpse in the fish). However the flood is subordinated in the illustration to the prediction of an imminent crisis in church and state, linked to the danger of a peasant rebellion.

Saturn was said to rule over lowly professions and occupations, such as rural workers, criminals, the diseased and the crippled. Saturn himself is frequently depicted as an aged cripple with a sickle or scythe, and it is clearly he who is intended by the figure holding the scythe and banner at the head of his peasant followers. The emperor, pope, cardinal and bishops opposing them stand for the children of Jupiter. The astrological significance of other planets in the conjunction underlines the threat of war and disorder implicit in the aggressive stance of the followers of Saturn. The moon represents changeability and restlessness, and is an unfavourable influence when in the sign of the fish. The Sun may stand for contentiousness, while Mars, the constant companion of Saturn, is the planet of war, standing for murder, violence, arson and theft. Venus is the counterforce to Mars, and represents morals, manners and fair behaviour, which are threatened by war [*Strauss, 1936: 20-36*]. These astrological allusions to the chaos resulting from the 'Great Conjunction' are reinforced by the presence of the two figures with pipe and drum in the background. These refer possibly to the folk belief that the sound of pipe and drum presage the imminence of war [*Bächtold-Stäubli, 1927-42: Vol. 6, 1596; Vol. 8, 1171*]. This is confirmed by the comet (shaped like a star, but given a comet's tail by rounded cross-strokes) to the left of these figures. According to Reynmann the advent of a comet in this year would bring a peasant rebellion with it. Saturn's banner and the band of armed peasants at his back confirm and complete all these allusions.

Images of the Peasant 43

Practica vber die grossen vnd ma=
nigfeltigen Coniunction der Planeten/die im
Jar.M.D.XXiiij.erscheinen/vñ vn=
gezweiffelt vil wunderbarlicher
ding geperen werden.

Auß Rö.Kay.May.Gnaden vnd Freyhaiten/Hüt sich menigklich/dyse meine Practica in zwayen Jaren nach zütrucken/bey verlierung.4.Marck lötigs Golds.

L. *Reynmann,* Practica uber die grossen und manigfeltigen Conjunction der Planeten die im MDXXIII jar erschienen, 1523,
Nuremberg: H. *Höltzel.* British Library C.71.h.14 (17).

Illustration 8

Prophetic and millenarian writings seem to have prepared the popular mind for the possibility of some inversion of the existing order, for 'the world turned upside down'. This expectation was vividly expressed in a 1508 prognostic showing the priests ploughing the fields and the peasants saying Mass [*von Bezold, 1890 : 147*]. Belief in astrology and cosmic fatalism served to keep alive the hope of such an inversion, and it found an appropriate image in the wheel of fortune, a stock genre picture of the time. The illustration reproduces the title-page of an anomymous pamphlet published in early May 1525, justifying the peasant revolt in terms of the right of resistance to ungodly authority. Addressed to 'the Assembly of Common Peasants of the German Nation', it stands close to the more radical ideas of the Swiss reformer Ulrich Zwingli, and may have been a reply to Luther's admonition to the peasants to obedience. It supplied biblical justification for the uprising, quoting among others Psalm 23: 'Though I walk through the valley of the shadow of death, I will fear no evil, for the Lord is with me . . .' The implications of its ideas were such that the civic authorities expelled its Nuremberg printer, Jerome Höltzel.

On the right of the depiction the pope, clad in armour, rides up on the wheel, behind him his supporters, armed cardinals, bishops and knights. These are identified by the inscription as the Romanists and Sophists, stock Lutheran epithets for the papalists and scholastic theologians. The wheel is turned by the figure of Dame Fortune. On the other side stand 'Peasants and Good Christians', clad as *Landsknechte* and armed with pikes and spears, onto whose upraised points the turn of the wheel will deposit the pope. The subtitle 'Who increases the Swiss? The greed of the lords' refers to the Swiss as the symbol of those who overthrew overwheening authority. The Swiss confederation of sturdy farmers allied with independent towns who threw off the yoke of feudal lords was a model both looked to by the peasants and feared by the princes. The Swiss were also used in the prophetic literature, the late-fifteenth century astrologer Johann Lichtenberger using much the same words to prophesy the spread of Swiss republicanism because the rulers would not moderate their behaviour [*Schottenloher, 1922 : 112*]. The illustration invokes this note of prophetic retribution, but the central subtitle preserves the uncertainty befitting the wheel of fortune theme, in which it was never sure where the wheel would come to rest: 'Here is the hour and time of the wheel of fortune. God knows who will remain supreme'.

Images of the Peasant

An die versamlung gemayner Pawer-
schafft/so in Hochteütscher Nation/vnd vil ande
rer ort/mit empörung vñ auffrür entstandē.ᛋc̄.
oB jr empörung billicher oder vnpillicher ge
stalt geschehe/ vnd was sie der Oberkait
schuldig oder nicht schuldig seind.ᛋc̄.
gegründet auß der heyligen Göt-
lichen geschrifft/ von Oberlen-
dischen mitbrüdern gütter
maynung aufgangen
vnd beschriben.ᛋc̄.

Hie ist des Glückradts stund vnd zeyt
Gott wayst wer der oberist bleybt.

An die versamlung gemayner Pawerschafft, so in Hochteütscher Nation, und vil
anderer ort, mit empörung und auffrur entstanden . . ., 1525.
Reproduced from Schottenloher, 1922; III.

Illustration 9

This reproduces a broadsheet published during the latter part of 1525, setting out the castles and abbeys 'attacked and plundered' by the peasants in the Black Forest, Franconian and Würzburg areas. The extensive list draws attention to the main objects of militant peasant rebellion. Castles and (mostly fortified) abbeys were seen as the seat of those evils which the peasants wished to have abolished. However the attitude to these visible signs of lordship was very different among various groups of peasants. The more moderate, such as the Union of Memmingen, welcomed the 'Christian Lords' among themselves, and demanded only that no supplies and ammunition be stored and the artillery dismantled. The more radical Black Forest troops demanded the demolition of all such seats of feudal control. The long list of those destroyed or pillaged before the end of April 1525 indicates that the radicals were quite successful during the victorious period of the war. Some 23 monasteries and the same number of castles in the Black Forest, and some 20 castles in Franconia are listed.

The woodcut is that from the title-page of the published sermon of the Peasant of Wöhrd, now used in a work hostile to the peasants. This illustrates the strength and pervasiveness of the image created by Karsthans, and its considerable development during the period 1521-25. The peasant with the flail is now intended to invoke not the evangelical lay-preacher, but the militant man of action, the peasant rebel. Had this shift of emphasis come from the peasant himself, it might have represented a change in the level of his political consciousness. Coming from his opponents, it pointed to the future and the fading of the positive image of the peasant. This image of the early years of the Reformation was now to be replaced by that of the disobedient subject.

Images of the Peasant

Das seind die Clöster vnd Schlösser/so die Schwartzweldischen Pawern verprent vnd geplundert haben.

Das seyn die Clöster.

Odassenhawsen.
Schussenried.
Zwisalten.
Mergendal.
Rodt.
Rockenburg.
Elchingen.
Bodenhawsen.
Olperg.
Saw.
Wingarten.
Haind.
Hebbach.
Gnederesell.
Bettenbrunnen.
Salmerschweyl.
Drenwepler.
Solgemo. ——Langnew
Schönpiren.
Herler.
Zucham.
Ebentral—— Lementhal
Hoffedi:m p:obst.

Das seind die Schlösser.

Emerlingen
Stadion.
Dorenweyler. Schloß.
Schemelberg.
Simendingd.
Graff Hansen/dissen vn ander met
Nimburg.
Her: Hansen vnd Caspar vō Langē
burg. 2. Schlösser.
Hessen vō Logenberg· vñ hern Wolf
Gerbling. 2. Schloß verpient.
Lauphaym verpient.
Allendo:ff.
Manstedten.
Altedten. als erschlagen.
Sinermankhawsen.
Onsenhawsen.
Schwendion.
Herr Hansen Bren võ Dremestigen.
Herr Jörg Drugkfessen dem haben
die Lindawer verpient Walpurg.
Thubing.
Tiglen des herren von Tremang.
Malou.

O ß ist alles vor dem April geschehen.

Im land zü Francken haben der Hell der Schwartz der Picht Bawren bauff dyse Clöster vnd Schlösser auß brenne vnd geplundert.

Die Clöster.

Prumpach.
Schwartzach.
Seligtal.
Grunach.
Helbechsen.
Pulicka.
Holtzkirch.
Oschin.
Terlosen.
Eberach.
Manckstetten.
Westerwinckel.
Derres

Die Schlösser.

Homeck.
Lauda.
Galachaym.
Obermergenthumb.
Weynlperg.
Reychelsperg.
Waltsen.
Einthaym.
Scheurenberg.
Newenhawß.
Budthardt.
Newenstat an der Irch vnd sonst. 5.
schlösser. Haylpum. Damffen.

Vnd daß das Wirtzpurgrisch vnd Brandenburgrisch hör sollen zü samen ziehen/in mainug kain Schloß noch Cloßter zü bleiben lassen/vnd auch keyn zoll zü gedulden. Alle waisser vnd holtz frey zü haben/vnd sind im willen zü ne ben auff Berelshoffen/Zabelein/Werhaur/vñ auff onser Frawen perg zü Wirtzburg. Also bald die bayd Stiffe Werg vnd Wirtzburg vmbgefallen sein vnd erobert von den Pawern/vñ der Bischoff zü Strassburg Stathalter im Schloß zü Ascherburg belegert/vñd im. 1 Schiff mit qui genomen worden vnd hat die Wirnburgisch landschafft tagraysung abge- schriben. Vnd empörten sich zü gleicherweys die vnterfassen zü der Newenstat an der Wsch. Do flichen die versagte Paw- ren us Gessing zü dem hauffen im Rich/die Otingen belegert oñ erobert habñ mit zwayen Craussen. Auch haben sy das Schloß zü Elbang auß picint.

Anno. M.D.XXV.

Das seind die Clöster, und Schlösser, so die Schwartzweldischen Pawren verprent
und geplundert haben, 1525. *Reproduced from Pianzola, 1961: 105.*

REFERENCES

Bächtold-Stäubli, H., 1927–42, *Handwörterbuch des deutschen Aberglaubens*, Berlin-Leipzig.

Bezold, F. von, 1890, *Geschichte der deutschen Reformation*, Berlin.

Clemen, O., 1902, *Beiträge zur Reformationsgeschichte*, Berlin.

Clemen, O., 1910, *Flugschriften aus den ersten Jahren der Reformation*, IV, Leipzig.

Engels, F., 1956, *The Peasant War in Germany*, Moscow Publishing House.

Hegg, P., 1954, 'Die Drucke der "Göttlichen Mühle" von 1521', *Schweizerisches Gutenbergmuseum*, XL.

Hind, A. M., 1963, *An Introduction to a History of Woodcut*, I, New York.

Ivins, W. M., 1969, *Prints and Visual Communication*, Cambridge, Mass.

McLuhan, M., 1964, *Understanding Media*, London.

Merker, P. (ed.), 1918, *Thomas Murners Deutsche Schriften*, IX, Strassburg.

Pianzola, M., 1961, *Bauern und Kunstler*, Berlin.

Radbruch, R. M., 1961, *Der deutsche Bauernstand zwischen Mittelalter und Neuzeit*, Göttingen.

Schottenloher, K., 1922, *Flugblatt und Zeitung*, Berlin.

Steinmann, U., 1960, 'Die Bundschuh-Fahnen des Joss Fritz', *Deutsches Jahrbuch für Volkskunde*, VI: 2.

Strauss, H. A., 1926, *Der astrologische Gedanke in der deutschen Vergangenheit*, Berlin-Munich.

Uhrig, K., 1936, 'Der Bauer in der Publizistik der Reformation bis zum Ausgang des Bauernkrieges', *Archiv für Reformationsgeschichte*, XXXIII.

Precursors of the Peasant War: 'Bundschuh' and 'Armer Konrad'—Popular Movements at the Eve of the Reformation

Adolf Laube*

This paper, originally prepared for the now defunct Concepts and Terms section, describes the major peasant movements in late fifteenth century South-Western Germany. These riots and rebellions prepared the way for the great confrontation of the mass movement of the 1524-26 Peasant War. The author points out that they have to be analyzed in the context of growing crisis and dissatisfaction all over Central Europe. In spite of their defeat the conspiratory movements and open uprisings had a significant rôle in preparing the ground for the armed struggle.

Bundschuh and Armer (poor) Konrad were both signs and designations which the urban and rural poor used to describe, in the symbolical way so typical of the Middle Ages, their contrast with and opposition to the ruling class: the nobility, the urban patricians and the clergy. Bundschuh was the poor man's footwear, made of rough rawhide, reaching up to the calf and bound to the leg criss-crosswise with long leather strips. As an expression of the poverty of the peasants and in contrast to the boot and spurs of the nobles, it acquired in the fifteenth century an additional symbolic significance, due to the additional meanings of the word Bund, i.e., literally a binding, but also binding together, bundle, hence—union. (Thus the translator of Engels' book on *The Peasant War in Germany*, in one of its widely read editions, caught the secondary meaning by choosing the expression 'union shoe', but seems to have missed the original reference to the poor man's footwear.) The Bundschuh first became a symbol of the peasant and urban poor in revolt at the Upper Rhine in the first part of the fifteenth century, appearing on the rebellious peasants' banners in 1439. Afterwards, up to the time of the Peasant War the Bundschuh was to be seen again and again, painted or embroidered on flags or as a real shoe on top of a pole signifying the unity of protesting commoners and as a symbol of conspiratory rebellion against the rich. Major Bundschuh-uprisings are known to have occurred, in 1493, 1502, 1513 and 1517.

Armer Konrad originates in the personal name Kunz, a diminutive of Konrad. This name was used in a derogatory manner by nobles and patricians for 'poor fellow' and was then taken up by the oppressed them-

*Head of Department, Central Institute for History, Academy of Sciences of the German Democratic Republic, Berlin.

selves as a kind of status designation in opposition to the lords in town and country. The leaders of a wide spread uprising in 1514 against the rule of Duke Ulrich of Wurttemberg called themselves 'Poor Conrad' or 'Poor Kunz'; the name was adopted by the entire movement. This expression has many parallels in countries at different times, where peasants also accepted the nicknames given to them by the lords and turned them into identifying slogans. In 1358 in France the peasants picked up the derogatory expression 'Jacques Bonhomme' given to them by the seigneurs during the great uprising of the Jacquerie.

There were many causes for popular movements such as the *Bundschuh* and the *Armer Konrad*. The results of the agrarian crisis of the fourteenth and fifteenth centuries not only affected the rural population but many feudal lords as well. On the other hand the growth of urban markets created new demands for goods. The development of territorial principalities, the change to mercenary armies and the continuous feudal wars also increased the demand for money. Therefore the lords attempted to increase their income by turning the screw on peasant dues and taxes.

The extent and nature of this increased feudal exploitation varied in the numerous German territories according to the differences in their agrarian structure, the development of commodity production and political conditions. Hardest hit were the peasants of the south-western areas, where the innumerable petty lordships conserved extremely mixed legal and land-tenure systems and where relationships between town and country were close because of the high degree of urbanization. In the estates of Swabia, in the south-western Black Forest, and in Upper Alsace, serfdom was strictly enforced or reintroduced, rights to tenancies curtailed, feudal dues increased and access to the commons reduced. Added to these increases in feudal oppression and the growing dependance on urban markets were the consequences of population growth and the sharpening of internal differentiation in the villages which in the late fifteenth century were particularly felt in the South-West. These factors brought middle- and small-holding peasants face to face with the menace of rapid pauperization (see below, p. 68 ff.).

The immediate causes of the uprisings were often local abuses in the legal and judicial system, new kinds of taxes and tolls, hardship caused by rampant usury or moral indignation over the irreligious and dissolute life of the clergy. The programme of the first major *Bundschuh* revolt in 1439 in the area of Schlettstadt in Alsace, reflects this very well. It demanded changes in the legal system, the expulsion of usurers, the abolition of the monasteries and of multiple benefices among the clergy and the limitation of taxes, dues and tolls. The conspirators, led by Jakob Hanser, a beadle (*scultetus*) from Bischweiler (a village belonging to the Crown), planned an uprising with the help of the Swiss Confederates, but were soon discovered and the organization was destroyed by the alarmed authorities. While this movement was primarily based on wealthier peasants, the ensuing conspiracies included more and more of the rural poor. They seem to have been

Precursors of the Peasant War

the main participants in the *Bundschuh* of 1502 which was organized by a young serf, Joss (Joseph) Fritz from Untergrombach near Bruchsal. This 'model conspirator'—as Engels called him—successfully combined the strong religious feelings of his fellow peasants with the needs of anti-feudal action. The programme of the 1502 *Bundschuh* called for the abolition of all oppression and an end to all lordship and authority on the basis of 'divine justice'. Serfdom was to be abolished, abbeys and monasteries dissolved, all ecclesiastical property distributed. No rent or tithe, no tax or toll or any other dues were to be paid ever again. Waters, meadows and woods were to be common to all and free to be used by everybody. The central theme was: 'Nothing but the justice of God'. This call for divine justice implied, objectively speaking, a programme for the overthrow of the existing order and its replacement by a new society based on the commands of the Bible (see below, pp. 54-62). The antifeudal movement became revolutionary.

The uprising, planned for April 1502, was, however, betrayed and the *Bundschuh* subdued, but the feudal lords were deeply disturbed by the conspiracy. The princes of the area held joint consultations about the suppression of similar outbreaks and even the emperor, Maximilian I, intervened and demanded the harshest punishment for the participants and their accomplices.

Joss Fritz, who managed to escape the disaster, organized a new *Bundschuh* in 1513, around Lehen in Breisgau, further upstream along the Rhine. Although the basic tenor of the programme remained that of 1502, Fritz combined fundamental demands for a new society with a number of reform proposals which were apt to appeal to wider circles of the urban and rural population. But only a few days before the set date for the open uprising, a conspirator confessed the plan to his priest and most of the participants were arrested, tortured and punished. A few, including Joss Fritz, escaped.

Unrest among the people, however, was not to be subdued as easily as that. Building on the widespread dissatisfaction which existed, Fritz set out to organize yet another *Bundschuh* in early 1517. This time he intended to reach beyond a limited area and tried to include the entire Upper Rhine. Centred around Strasbourg, on both sides of the river, the threads of the conspiracy reached as far as Lower Alsace and Baden. The rural poor and the urban-plebeian elements were more than ever before included in this union, together with uprooted beggars and vagrants. The programme contained the same demand for a total transformation of society and polity, but an important innovation was that common action of the poor in town and countryside was emphasized. Although Joss Fritz observed all the rules of underground organization, even this—his greatest conspiracy—was discovered and destroyed.

The memory of the *Bundschuh* stayed alive however, and continued to inspire peasant fighters in the battles of the Peasant War. But it is remarkable that even in conditions of general crisis and dissatisfaction and with such a splendid organizer as the 'model-conspirator' Joss Fritz, these 'secret societies' were unable to avoid the relatively crude methods of detection and oppression. The successes of the authorities, as well as the recurrent experience of defeat of the most courageous radical elements, must have played a role in increasing the bitterness that finally led to the great Peasant War of 1524-26.

Less revolutionary and anti-feudal in character was the uprising of the 'Poor Conrad' in Wurttemberg. The revolt started over the levy of a new tax. Owing to the maladministration and lavish court expenses of the tyrannical Duke Ulrich, the duchy was so deeply in debt that regular income did not even cover the interest. This had to be remedied by a new consumer's tax on foodstuffs which triggered a spontaneous rebellion in the district of Schrondorf in the Remstal. The movement spread fast, peasant revolt joined hands with urban unrest and by June 1514 the whole duchy was aflame. The urban ruling groups, which played an important role in Wurttemberg and had tried to use the uprising to strengthen their power in the duchy, became now the main object of the attack. But an alliance between the Duke and his patriciate succeeded in quenching the rebellion, partly by compromise, partly—as in the core area of Schorndorf—by armed force.

Bundschuh and *Armer Konrad* were the most important popular movements on the eve of the Reformation and the Peasant War. However, they were not the only ones. More or less localized or regional peasant uprisings broke out in great numbers during these decades. Also two waves of urban movements swept over Germany in the 1470-80s and between 1509 and 1514, which clearly surpassed the usual recruitment city riots of the later Middle Ages. Uprisings and strikes of miners in the major mining district, territorial princes, marked the beginning of struggles in the industrial sphere. The so-called anti-monopolistic movements against the take-over of great segments of the economy by the new companies—the Fuggers, the Welsers, the Hochstetters, etc.—and their new, ruthless business practices were supported by many and very diverse social groups. Finally there was dissent and opposition of many kinds, beginning with the social critique of the Humanists, the *gravamina* against the Roman curia, the fears of the superstitious masses of apocalyptic catastrophies and the bitter fights among princes and lords around the question of the 'reform of the Empire'.

It is in this general context that *Bundschuh* and *Armer Konrad* have their historical significance. They were expressions of a deep social crisis at the threshold of the transition from feudalism to capitalism, in which all classes and social groups experienced a process of dislocation and differentiation of unprecedented extent, and which also caused grave difficultities for the ruling classes. The resulting popular movements clearly reflect the extremely complex social conditions of the period with the many forms of oppositional forces pursuing very specific aims and interests. Although some of the *Bundschuh* rebellions show attempts at a generalization of complaints and a formulation of a wide coalition of all disenfranchised elements, all the uprisings up to 1517 remained both regionally and socially limited. This enabled the rulers to liquidate them one by one. However, they deepened the existing contradictions between social progress and political oppression and thus prepared the ground for the revolutionary mass movement of the early bourgeois revolution.

NOTE

The basic source material has been collected and edited by A. Rosenkranz, *Der Bundschuh. Die Erhebungen des südwestdeutschen Bauernstandes in den Jahren 1493–1517*, 2 vols. (Heidelberg, 1927), and H. Oehler 'Der Aufstand des Armen Konrad 1514', *Württembergische Vierteljahrshefte* 38 (1932) 401–486. For the symbolism important is: U. Steinmann 'Die Bundschuhfahnen des Joss Fritz', *Deutsches Jahrbuch für Volkskunde*, (1960) 243–284. The general context of these uprisings is now discussed in A. Laube, M. Steinmetz, G. Vogler, *Illustrierte Geschichte der deutschen frühbürgerlichen Revolution*, (Berlin, 1974). Valuable and exhaustive is the monograph G. Franz, *Der deutsche Bauernkrieg* 10th ed. (Darmstadt, 1975). The translation referred to above (p. 49) is that of M. J. Olgin, International Publishers: New York 1926, now repr. in F. Engels, *The German Revolutions*, ed. L. Krieger (Chicago, 1967).

'Old Law' and 'Divine Law' in the German Peasant War

Heide Wunder*

The paper treats the two core concepts of the Peasant War in the form of a report on the present state of research on law and social conflict in the late Middle Ages. The author attempts to outline a history of the meaning of the terms, based on the results of legal, constitutional and religious historians. The complex method of inquiry is particularly significant and may very well serve as a model for comparative studies of similar but different ideas of legitimation for revolts. Her tentative results suggest the necessity of revision of many hitherto uncritically accepted simplifications and promises to open up new vistas through in-depth analysis of the terminology of the rebellious peasants.

Günther Franz, author of the still widely read and accepted book on the Peasant War [*1933*] was the first to contrast the function of 'old law' (*altes Recht*) and 'divine law' (*göttliches Recht*) in the Peasant War. Franz saw the Peasant War as the result of a long series of peasant revolts which, from the late thirteenth century onwards, were fought under the slogan of return to 'old law' or 'old custom' (*Herkommen*) or with the justification by 'divine law'. While the revolts for the restitution of ancient custom were characterized by spontaneous local outbursts with wide popular participation, the uprisings for 'divine justice' (*göttliche Gerechtigkeit*) of the *Bundschuh*-type [see above, 49-53] were prepared by organized conspiracies and tended to be overregional. All the major complaints of the Peasant War were raised in these precursors of the great conflict: the economic oppression and legal insecurity caused by the lords' new claims to higher rents, dues and suits of court as well as the imposed dominion of the formerly autonomous village by territorial lords who could not provide the services of peacekeeping and so on, to the community. Franz therefore described the Peasant War as a 'conflict between corporative popular law (*genossenschaftliches Volksrecht*) and authoritative seigneurial law (*Herrschaftsrecht*)' [*1975 : 291*]. He attributed the expansion of the local and regional revolts into the great Peasant War to the impact of the Lutheran Reformation. The 'new Gospel' offered the peasants an effective justification in which the slogan 'divine law' acquired mass appeal. 'The Reformation bridged the gap between old law and divine law' [*1970 : 137*].

*Department of History, University of Hamburg, Federal Republic of Germany. The author wishes to express her thanks for references and assistance to Professor Rainer Wohlfeil and Dr. Achatz von Müller.

The novelty of this assessment lies in the combination of two hitherto independent lines of inquiry: medieval legal and constitutional history and Reformation history. Franz's notion of the old law was based on the characterization of medieval Germanic law by Fritz Kern [*1919*]. 'Law is old', law is good', 'good old law is unenacted *(ungesetzt*[1]*)* and unwritten' and 'all law comes from God', were the maxims that seemed to be instrumental in describing and understanding both positive laws (as recorded in customals and charters) and the peasants' concept of right and law. Since customary law differed from estate to estate, peasant resistance against its misuse was limited to a definite lordship, and so the uprisings for the restitution of old law were legitimate only within certain boundaries. The revolts based on justification by divine law, however, were able to transcend such limitations and proceed to a virtual demand for 'general liberation of the peasantry' [*Franz 1933 : 73*]. The historian of the *Bundschuh* [*Rosenkranz, 1927*] drew parallels between these movements and the English revolt of 1381 and also the Hussites in order to show the significance of religious movements in making the peasantry revolutionary.

Although the recourse to divine justice already lent these precursory revolts a programme of general reconstruction of society, polity, economy and religious life based on the Bible—which went well beyond their definite material demands—Franz recognized in the mass movement of the Peasant War a qualitative change in the meaning of divine law as a consequence of the Reformation.

Critics of the dichotomy of old vs. divine law, among them Nipperdey and Melcher [*1966 : 623*] point out that Franz overlooked divine justification as an element of the medieval concept of law as presented by his own authority [*Kern, 1919*]: old law was always considered divine as well. Peter Blickle [*1975 : 135-143*], a pupil of Franz, retains the notion of two sets of legitimation, but orders them into a sequence. Only after the failure of claims based on old custom did the peasants find it necessary to turn to divine law, since it promised successful resistance to the lords under the novel conditions of the early sixteenth century. The slogans of the *Bundschuh* based on divine justice *(Gerechtigkeit Gottes)* do not appear to him as important as they did to his mentor. Blickle's attempt at a detailed analysis of events related to the attitudes of peasants and the actual meaning of 'divine justice' in different circumstances is very valuable. Yet another interpretation of old law vs. divine law was recently proposed by Günter Vogler [*1975 : 220-221*], who emphasized the complementary function of the two ideas of legitimation, based on his analysis of the Twelve Articles.

These controversies will probably be best resolved by local and regional research into the chronological and spatial pattern of revolts based on the one or the other system of legitimation. The results of this would offer insights into the transition from the cries for restitutions of old custom to the reception of divine law in the context of the 'evangelical', i.e., Lutheran demands of 1525. Two examples may suggest the interrelationship of these two sets of ideas. As early as 1513, Joss Fritz, while organizing the *Bundschuh* around

Lehen, used this formulation in a propaganda address: '... if you really want to help us and help divine justice, you have to be silent and tell nobody about it. You see how badly off we are and that we are not left to live according to our old usages, rights and customs' [*Rosenkranz 1927: 1,187*]. This argument does not quite support Blickle's scepticism about the importance of the *Bundschuh*. However, the evidence from the peasant revolt in the Samland (Prussia) seems to support Blickle's propositions about the relative function of the two slogans. Old law, as recorded in their village charters and confirmations thereof, granted the Samland peasants individual and collective rights of complaint, even of passive resistance against novel exactions. However, the slogan of divine justice and the reference to the Holy Gospel proved to be exactly the right means for peasant self-help against an 'ungodly' magistrate, because it raised the resistance from a matter of self-interest to one of general interest, of 'common weal' [*Wunder, 1975 : 34-35*]. This seems to be a good case of divine law serving as the legitimation of the common man's right to resistance (*Widerstandsrecht*).

The main trends of recent scholarship then are to criticize, correct and complement Franz's results, either by more subtle analysis of the primary sources or by applying new theoretical premises, such as those of an early-bourgeois revolution. Little new has been done to widen the basis of information through the discovery and study of additional sources or to consider relevant results from other historical disciplines regarding the notions of law. Traditional cooperation with legal and ecclesiastical historians seems to have broken down, due to the increased concern with the social and economic aspects of the Peasant War. Thus, in spite of considerable new scholarship on this period, it is still true that an inquiry into the development of the meaning (*Begriffsgeschichte*) of the terms 'divine law', 'divine justice' and 'justice of God' is lacking [*Blickle 1975 : 141*]. This applies also to the notion of 'old law', at any rate as far as German territories are concerned.[2]

It is unlikely that these gaps will be filled soon, considering the complexity of the issue, the scarcity of special monographs[3] and the present high standards set for such social histories of concepts [*Koselleck 1972 : 116-131*]. Valuable guidelines were, however, offered by Griewank [*1973*], who discussed medieval notions of law and order as an introduction to his investigation of the modern concept of revolution. In this study, the close links between secular and spiritual elements within the ideas about old and divine law, and their manifold relationships to the right to resistance are neatly presented, together with their different uses and effects in various political, social and intellectual contexts.

In attempting to draw the outlines of a history of these concepts one can also build on the results of historians of constitution, law and the Church, hitherto mostly neglected outside their specific fields. These approaches, of course, treat the notions of 'old law' and 'divine law' in the framework of their respective disciplines, but this fact may be quite useful for our purpose, because it suggests the width and variety of meanings and keeps us from proceeding on too narrow a gauge.

Otto Brunner's basic and innovatory study on the relationship of power and right in German constitutional development [*1939*] retained Kern's notion of a 'good, old and divine law' as the basis of his assessment of medieval legal thought. This 'ancient unity of law and justice', i.e., of the idea of law, normative laws and subjective, individual rights, appeared to him as the core of medieval lordship and the prerequisite for the right to resistance in the form of armed self-help against any trespass of law and right. Brunner distinguished two processes of disintegration of this complex medieval unity. A 'contradiction between the norms of Christian moral conduct and actual social practice, particularly that of personal unfreedom and serfdom (*Leibherrschaft*)' seems to have been perceived as early as the eleventh century. A decisive turning point for him is the *Reformatio Sigismundi*, which already heralded the 'break between old law and divine law as represented by the revolutionary movements of the late Middle Ages' [*1965 : 138*]. Brunner then dates the other major step, i.e., the divorce of the idea of right from positive law, which essentially strengthened the rise of the sovereign state over particular lordships, with reference to Jean Bodin, into the sixteenth century. These theses demonstrate the significance of constitutional development for deciding the actual contents and functions of the systems of legitimation such as old law and divine law.

Recent research in legal history has questioned the validity of Kern's [*1919*] unitary concept of medieval law from different points of view. His confining of the medieval idea of right to the field of Germanic continuity, of unwritten customary law and of its basis in the legal perception of the people have been challenged. K. Kroeschell [*1968*] and G. Köbler [*1971*] have demonstrated several layers and types of early and high medieval law, differences in their validity and recurrent impacts of late ancient and ecclesiastical notions of law and right in the crucial epochs of German legal development. They point out, *inter alia*, that the central notion of 'custom' does not go back beyond the twelfth century, when it evolved in the course of an 'early reception' of Roman and Canon Law. The twofold legitimation by 'ancient custom' and 'divine law' appeared likewise in the twelfth century. K. von See arrived at very similar results in his studies of Scandinavian legal development, which used to be the showpiece for Germanic continuity: 'There is little and only rather late evidence for the idea of *Volksrecht*, 'customary law' and 'good old law' and they seem to have emerged under more or less ecclesiastical influence' [*1964 : 102*]. G. Theuerkauf pointed to another shortcoming of Kern's definition: 'Attempts at extensive recording of laws, such as those of Charlemagne and the Hohenstaufen, do not tally well with Kern's theory. Kern was right in stressing the overwhelming role of customary law, particularly in the early and the high middle ages, but the function of recording the law has to be re-examined. It is not sufficient to dispose of written law just as customary law written up' [*1968 : 26*].

Consideration of meanings and function of law [*Krause, 1958*] contrasts old law with the great bulk of new law [*Sprandel, 1962*], both private and seigneurial. Krause goes so far as to state: 'medieval law had to be preferably new' [*1958 : 211*]. But this new law had relatively weak validity, because it was bound to the lifetime of the law-giver. Confirmations and renewals could lend a lasting quality and let it become old law, with all the implications of the latter. But also 'good old law' was subject to change by improvement: good became better. However, the notion of novelty and innovation was suspect for the medieval legal mind and therefore preferably avoided. New attitudes to law emerged gradually from the twelfth century onwards under the impact of Roman and Canon jurisprudence and by the sixteenth century were essentially accepted everywhere. The difference in validity of old law and new law waned or even got reversed insofar as new law became more highly valued than old.

Already the intermediate results of these studies suggest a significant tension between the many layers and meanings of positive law on the one hand and the tendency to preserve the unity of law in legal thinking on the other. This tension was clearly manifest in the Peasant War: not only did the peasants refer to the old law, but the lords secular and spiritual did so too (*Blickle, 1975 : 134*). Of course, the peasants had their traditional customs in mind, while the seigneurs thought of their chartered privileges. Still, this demonstrates how one-sided it is to charge the peasants of 1525 with 'traditionalism' and 'conservatism'.

Novelty and innovation, religious, social and political alike, were regarded as 'rebellious', 'seditious' and 'heretical', and hence all attempts at change were given out as 'improvements' or 'reform' of the original (good) order of things and were so perceived in the mind of medieval man. Under the conditions of the late fifteenth and early sixteenth centuries the peasant whose position was threatened by secular and spiritual landlords (*Grundherren*) and territorial lords, could not in fact resort to any legitimate appeal other than the old law. Otherwise their attempts to preserve their status would have been labelled innovation (although they did not completely escape this charge).

Last but not least, the appeal to the old law was also an expression of the political and legal powerlessness of the peasantry. While nobles and cities could legally press for their demands by the threat of violence [*Brunner, 1965 : 50-73*], 'poor folk' could only submit their grievances humbly, but had no right of resistance; no legitimate positive action was granted them.

Two main concepts of divine law (*ius divinum, lex Dei, iustitia Dei*) have been studied by legal historians: divine law as an expression of the sacredness (*Heiligkeit*) of ancient Germanic law [*Kern, 1919*] and as the central category in canon law for the divine order in general and the precepts of the Old and New Testaments in particular. Church historians have studied the connections between the Christian ideas of natural law and divine law and also the emergence of the slogan of divine justice in the religious movements of the High Middle Ages. Like the 'apostolic life' (*vita apostolica*) as the programme of the earlier heresies [*Grundmann, 1961 : 13 ff, 504 ff*], the notion of divine law had a very wide spectrum of use from the official hierarchy down to heterodox lay movements. Rosenkranz [1927 : 314] observed that by the fifteenth century 'divine law' had acquired unfavourable connotations with the authorities. However, Brunner [1965 : 134] quotes several instances where divine and old law were mentioned together by rulers and ruled alike. More studies using the numerous existing text editions are needed to be able to follow up the history of the notion of divine law in the religious and secular reforming movements of the later Middle Ages.[4]

Two recent papers have drawn attention to hitherto neglected aspects. H. Oberman speaks of a 'Justice of God movement', the roots of which are supposed to be in urban community life, particularly in imperial free cities and late medieval city states, and which was conceived as 'common responsibility of all citizens to the will of God' [1974: 304]. The peasants who appealed to the justice of God had actually borrowed some of their demands, such as the right to elect their parish priests and other civil liberties, from urban programmes. Thus the Lutheran reformation reached a rural population which had been influenced by 'urban theology' for some two hundred years and therefore was prepared for the reform [Moeller, 1962]. Oberman also stresses the impact of the intellectual communication that accompanied urban-rural economic relationships as a key element in the study of the relationship between Reformation and Peasant War. He agrees, however, that the urban models had only a limited impact on seigneurial dependents, owing to their very different social, economic and political conditions.

While divine law could thus be incorporated into the structure of urban autonomy, historians tend to see the countryside as influenced primarily by Luther's domesticating theories on dominion. Recently, however, R. Brecht [1974] commented on this old problem of Reformation research [Scheible, 1969] while discussing the Twelve Articles in terms of the dichotomony of right to resistance vs. magisterial authority. He attempts to prove that the Lutheran interpretation of the Gospel, which he claims to be the main religious authority of the authors of the articles, does indeed contain the justification of resistance against an ungodly magistrate. The peasants' references to the holy Gospels and divine law were thus not misunderstandings—as Conze still sees it [1972: 411 ff]—but had their basis in Luther's own writings.[5]

In summary: the slogans of 'old law' and 'divine law' as expressions of a legitimizing ideology of the peasant war can only be correctly assessed if seen in the context of the history of law, constitution and religion. The aspect of social psychology of the active masses—probably analogous to Erikson's study of one protagonist [1958]—might also be added. In order to go beyond general statements about the extent of different meanings and functions of these core concepts, much more research is needed. Not only the medieval but also the early modern period needs to be included following the hints of G. Theuerkauf [1968] and E. Hölzle [1930]. This implies looking at popular movements from the comparative point of view as R. Hilton [1973] and G. Fourquin [1972] have done for the Middle Ages. Useful material has been accumulated by E. Le Roy Ladurie [1974] for France and some attempts have been made by Marxist historians. The scope of investigation should not be limited to peasant movements; urban movement (e.g., in the Low Countries) and the history of political thought (*ius divinum* theory) should not be neglected. The comparative aspect may get further impetus by considering the wider outlook which E. Hobsbawm recently presented [*1972*]. The scope of the inquiry has to be widened to include all the ramifications of the basic terms and their legal validity, and the evidence has to be carefully classified in terms of time, origin and intentions. Such a study may arrive at a genuine social history of the meaning of these terms, which in turn may offer a means to answer such basic questions as: Was the Peasant War a revolution? If so, what was the character of this revolution? Was it a political or an 'early-bourgeois' revolution? Was it a 'revolution of the common man' (Blickle) or a 'system-conflict between the common man and his lord' (Wohlfeil)?

NOTES

[1] The contrast with modern legislation and its statutes (*Gesetz*) should be noted.
[2] General considerations of this theme for a number of European centuries have been presented by Gagnér (*1960*).
[3] Useful studies have been published by Schmidt (*1939*); Michaelis (*1953*) and Günther (*1965*).
[4] See also Grundmann (*1967*); recent research in the German Democratic Republic is surveyed by Laube (*1970*) and Steinmetz (*1970*).
[5] A different interpretation is presented by Hoyer (*1975*).

REFERENCES

Blickle, P., 1975, *Die Revolution von 1525*, Munich.
Brecht, M., Der theologische Hintergrund der Zwolf Artikel, der Bauern in Schwaben von 1525', *Zeitschrift für Kirchengeschichte* 85: 30–64.
Brunner, O., 1939, *Land und Herrschaft*, Baden b. Wien, 5th ed. Darmstadt 1965.
Conze, W., 1972, 'Bauer', *Geschichtliche Grundbegriffe: Historisches Lexikon zur politisch-sozialen Sprache in Deutschland*, ed. O. Brunner, W. Conze, R. Koselleck, 1: A-D Stuttgart, 407–439.
Erikson, E., 1958, *Young Man Luther: A Study in Psychoanalysis and History*, New York.
Fourquin, G., 1972, *Les soulèvements populaires au Paris, Moyen age*, (Collection SUP, L'Historien 12).
Franz, G., 1933, *Der deutsche Bauernkrieg*, 10th ed. Darmstadt 1975.
Franz, G., 1970, *Geschichte des deutschen Bauernstandes vom frühen Mittelalter bis zum 19. Jahrhundert*, Stuttgart (Deutsche Agrargeschichte IV).
Gagnér, S., 1960, *Studien zur Ideengeschichte der Gesetzgebung*, Uppsala: Acta Univ. Upsall. Studia Iuridica Ups. 1.
Griewank, K., 1973, *Der neuzeitliche Revolutionsbegriff. Entstehung und Geschichte*, enlarged edition *1955*, Frankfurt (suhrkamp taschenbuch wissenschaft 52).
Grundmann, H., 1961, *Religiöse Bewegungen im Mittelalter*, 2nd ed. Darmstadt.
Grundmann, H., 1967, *Ketzergeschichte des Mittelalters*, 2nd ed. Gœttingen. (Die Kirche in ihrer Geschichte, ed. K. D. Schmidt-E. Wolf 2, G).

Günther, G., 1965, ' "Altes Recht", "Göttliches Recht" und "Römisches Recht" in der Zeit der Reformation und des Bauernkrieges', *Wissenschaftliche Zeitschrift der Univ. Leipzig*, 14, Gesellschaft- und Sprachwiss, Reihe 13: 427–434.
Hilton, R., 1973, *Bond Men Made Free: Medieval Peasant Movements and the English Rising of 1381*. N.Y.
Hobsbawm, E. J., 1972, 'The Social Function of the Past', *Past & Present*, 55: 3–17.
Hölzle, E., 1931, *Das alte Recht und die Revolution. Eine politische Geschichte Württembergs in der Revolutionszeit 1789–1805*, Munich and Berlin.
Hoyer, S., 1975, 'Widerstandsrecht und Widerstandspflicht in der Flugschrift "An die versamlung gemayner pawerschafft" (1525)', in *Der Bauer im Klassenkampf: Studien zur Geschichte der bäuerlichen Klassenkämpfe im Spätfeudalismus* ed. G. Heitz et al. Berlin, 129–155.
Kern, F., 1919, 'Recht und Verfassung im Mittelalter', *Historische Zeitschrift* 120, 1–79. English translation by S. B. Chrimes: *Kingship and Law in the Middle Ages*, Oxford 1939. 149–205.
Köbler, G., 1971, *Das Recht im frühen Mittelalter*, Cologne-Vienna.
Koselleck, R., 1972, 'Begriffsgeschichte und Sozialgeschichte', *Soziologie und Sozialgeschichte. Aspekte und Probleme*, Opladen, 116–131. (=Kölner Zeitschrift für Soziologie, Sonderheft 16.)
Krause, H., 1958, 'Dauer und Vergänglichkeit im mittelalterlicheen Recht', *Zeitschrift der Savigny Stiftung für Rechtsgeschichte*. Germ. Abt. 75., 206–251.
Kroeschell, K., 1968, 'Recht und Rechtsbegriff im 12. Jh.' *Probleme des 12. Jahrhunderts. Reichenau-Vorträge 1965–67*, Constance, 309–335 (=Vorträge und Forschungen ed. T. Mayer 12.)
Laube, A. et al., 1970, 'Forschungen zur Geschichte des Mittelalters', *Historische Forschungen in der DDR 1960–1970. Analysen und Berichte. Zum XIII. Internationalen Historikerkongress in Moskau 1970*. Berlin.
Le Roy Ladurie, E., 1974, 'Über die Bauernaufstände in Frankreich' in *Wirtschaftliche und soziale Strukturen im säkularen Wandel*, Festschr. f. W. Abel zum 70. Geburtstag, ed. I. Bog et al., Bd. 1, Hanover, 277–305, and 'Révoltes et contestations rurales en France de 1675 à 1788', *Annales c.s.c.* 29 (1974), 6–22.
Michaelis, H., 1953, *Die Verwendung und Bedeutung der Bibel in den Hauptschriften der Bauern von 1525/26: Unter Berücksichtigung der bedeutendsten Reformentwürfe aus der Zeit des 15. Jahrhunderts* Thesis D. theol. Greifswald.
Moeller, B., 1962, *Reichsstadt und Reformation*, Gütersloh, (=Schriften des Vereins für Reformationsgeschichte, 180).
Nipperdey, T. and P. Melcher, 1966, 'Bauernkrieg', *Sowjetsystem und Demokratische Gesellschaft. Eine vergleichende Enzyklopädie* ed. C. D. Kernig et al., Freiburg, 1: 611–627.
Oberman, H., 1974, 'Tumultus rusticorum. Vom 'Klosterkrieg' zum Fürstensieg. Beobachtungen zum Bauernkrieg unter besonderer Berücksichtgung zeitgenossischer Beurteilungen', *Zeitschrift für Kirchengeschichte* 85: 301–16.
Rosenkranz, A., 1927, *Der Bundschuh. Die Erhebungen des südwestdeutschen Bauernstandes in den Jahres 1493–1517*, 2 vols., Heidelberg.
Scheible, H., ed. 1969, *Das Widerstandsrecht als Problem der deutschen Protestanten 1523–1546*, Gütersloh (=Texte zur Kirchen-und Theologiegeschichte 10).
Schmidt, I., 1939, *Das Göttliche Recht und seine Bedeutung im deutschen Bauernkrieg*, Zeulenroda.
See, K. von, 1964, *Altnordische Rechtswörter, Philologische Studien zur Rechtsauffassung und Rechtsgesinnung der Germanen*, Tübingen (=Hermaea. Germastische Forschungen N.I. 16).
Sprandel, R., 1962, 'Über das Problem des neuen Rechts im früheren Mittelalter', *Zeitschrift der Savigny Stiftung für Rechtsgeschichte* Kan. Abt. 48: 117–137.

Steinmetz, M., 1970, 'Forschungen zur Geschichte der Reformation und des deutschen Bauernkrieges', *Historische Forschungen* ... (see above, Laube 1970) ... 338–350.
Theuerkauf, G., 1968, '*Lex, Speculum, Compendium iuris. Rechtsaufzeichnungen und Rechtsbewusstsein in Norddeutschland vom 8. bis zum 16. Jahrhundert*, Cologne (= Forschungen zur deutschen Rechtsgeschichte 6).
Vogler, G., 1975, 'Der revolutionäre Gehalt und die räumliche Verteilung der oberschwäbischen Zwölf Artikel', *Revolte und Revolution in Europa*, ed. P. Blickle, Munich: 206–231 (= Historische Zeitschrift Beiheft, 4 N.F.).
Wunder, H., 1975, 'Zur Mentalität aufständischer Bauern. Möglichkeiten der Zusammenarbeit von Geschichtswissenschaft und Anthropologie, dargestellt am Beispiel des Samländischen Bauernaufstandes von 1525', Der Deutsche Bauernkrieg 1524–1526, ed. H.-U. Wehler, Göttingen, 9–37 (= Geschichte und Gesellschaft, Sonderheft 1).

The Economic, Social and Political Background of the Twelve Articles of the Swabian Peasants of 1525

Peter Blickle*

A quantitative and qualitative analysis of the local and regional documents of complaints, which served as the basis for the formulation of the influential Twelve Articles (see above, 14-18) permits the author to refine the assessment of the peasants' programme in 1525. Treating the main demands in three groups, he is able to show the nodes of conflict in the re-introduction of serfdom, the economic pressure on the peasant households and the burdens placed on them by the new territorial princes. Combining the textual evidence with demographic and economic analysis, he reveals the social conflicts within and around the South German peasant communities of the early sixteenth century. The plight of the peasants can thus be seen and the main lines of protest and resistance distinguished.

It is safe to assume that without the Twelve Articles of the peasants of Upper Swabia, the Peasant War, this spectacular event of the 'Reformation era' would have taken a different course. This famous document was a statement of complaints, a programme for reform and a political manifesto in one. It held together the revolution of 1525 like a clamp both in terms of matter and in terms of time. Formulated at the outset of the uprising in February-March 1525 the Twelve Articles appeared on the agenda of the Diet of Spires in 1526, months after the military defeat of the peasants. In barely two months 20 editions were printed and spread over the whole area of the uprising from Thuringia to Tyrol, from the Alsace to Salzburg. Cities, noblemen and clergy, who were induced to join one or other peasant troop had often to take an oath on the Twelve Articles.

In the last hundred years historians of the Peasant War have frequently asked the very legitimate question: what made these twelve paragraphs such an overwhelming success. Was it their moderate formulation, their preference for the Gospels, their revolutionary contents or their superregionally valid definition of the difficulties of the agrarian system and the peasant economy? However, no detailed investigation has been undertaken on the no doubt secondary but, as I shall try to demonstrate, highly relevant question of the document's social, economic and political background.

*The editor wishes to acknowledge the assistance of G. Scardellato (UBC) in the translation of this article—JMB.

The local and regional problems that served as raw material for the authors of the Twelve Articles, Sebatian Lotzer and Christoph Schappeler, have received only rather dilettante treatment, including a recent study by Ernst Walder [*1954*]. To get at least partially unequivocal answers to the concrete questions raised by the Twelve Articles one has to turn to the old, respectable and descriptive collections of sources, like that edited by Franz Ludwig Baumann [*1896*], or to the most recent studies based on modern methodology by David W. Sabean [*1972*]. Günter Vogler was quite right when he emphasized at an international symposium on the Peasant War held earlier this year in Memmingen, that 'the relationship between economic, social and political contents of the Twelve Articles needs further clarification' [*Vogler, 1975*].

There is good reason to assume that the main vestiges of feudalism in the agrarian sphere survived in essentially the same form in the different regions of the uprising. This assumption makes a detailed inquiry into the economic, social and political background of the Twelve Articles highly relevant for explaining the causes of the revolution of 1525 in terms of regional studies. Thus the crises of feudalism may be not only postulated but also analysed and defined by following up the complaints and demands that led to the formulation of the Twelve Articles.

The main demands contained in this document are, in brief: free election of parish priests, redistribution of the tithe, abolition of serfdom (*Leibeigenschaft*)[2] and heriot, freedom of hunting and fishing, restitution of woods, forests and commons (*Allmende*) to the communities, reduction of services and boonworks, re-evaluation of property, lowering of seigneurial dues and finally more legal protection and security on the basis of traditional law.

Leaving the first two articles about essentially ecclesiastical matters aside, the demands fall neatly into three general categories: serfdom, heriot and services belong to the first, hunting, fishing, woods and commons to the second and landlordship (*Grundherrschaft*) with its corollaries (like low justice) to the third. The Twelve Articles as we now know them were—as Günther Franz [*1939*] has convincingly demonstrated—an aggregate product based on the complaints of individual peasants, villages or estates of Upper Swabia. How representative were they of the grievances of the peasants? How far did they constitute the highest common denominator of the causes that led to the Peasant War? These questions can best be answered by investigating the local articles of complaints and qualifying them. This process will also permit us to make qualitative statements about the subjective priorities of the problems as perceived by the peasants. An additional inquiry into the question of how correctly this subjective consciousness reflected objective conditions, would be a first step toward an analysis of the casual factors of the revolution of 1525, as has been demanded by Thomas Nipperdey and Peter Melcher [*1973: 295*]. While the Twelve Articles show only incompletely the relative weight and dimension of the single grievances in the context of the entire collection of complaints, a statistical evaluation of the local and regional articles[3] can offer insights into these questions.

The third article demands *tout court* the abolition of serfdom. The significance of this question and its ramifications becomes apparent when we realize that 90 per cent of all peasants whose complaints are known to us, singled it out; in 24 out of 35 local and regional submissions it is listed in the first or second place. Among the servile obligations that of death duty (heriot) is most unequivocally disliked (37 per cent), while the complaints about fines (payed in recognition of servile status) are mentioned by 27 per cent and about constraints on marriage by 24 per cent. The demand for the abolition of other obligations connected with serfdom is relatively weak: only 11 per cent insist on it. These figures explain to a great extent, why the authors of the Twelve Articles found it necessary to mention heriot specifically (See above, Article XI: 17).

Complaints about the commons and related issues taken together appear in 81 per cent of the original lists. Preference is given to the demand for continuation or extension of wood supply (herbage) (61 per cent) and for rights to commons and pasture (46 per cent). The claim for restitution of communal rights to fishing, extensively presented in the Twelve Articles, had its basis in the local demands for limited or total freedom of fishing (27 per cent and 4 per cent respectively) and of the waters (26 per cent); two connected, if not identical demands, which together appear in more than half (52 per cent) of all local and regional documents. Much less importance seems to be placed on the hunting rights, since they are mentioned only by 20 per cent of the peasants.

All grievances regarding landlordship taken together suggest that this institution was also a major focus of crisis, with 83 per cent complaining about it. Many articles wish to see the rents (*Gülten*) reduced (72 per cent) and entrance fees at the transfer of holdings lowered (61 per cent). However, there does not seem to have been a unilateral increase of rents, etc., by the lords, as the peasants mostly maintain that the rents are high (39 per cent) but rarely that they have been raised (17 per cent). Connected to this is the relatively weak presence of complaints about the deterioration of property rights (15 per cent).

Only the heavy fines for 'major misdemeanours' and some new criminal statutes are criticized in the Twelve Articles, and these only rather briefly. The local and regional complaints show a much greater interest in legal matters, with 67 per cent of them containing some demand in this field. Heavy fines are mentioned relatively seldom (10 per cent), more frequently the practice of issuing new statutes (27 per cent), but most conspicuous are the remonstrances about the administration of justice (41 per cent). This quantitative summary of individual complaints suggests three major areas of tension:

1. Most of the basic conflicts are connected with serfdom, which placed heavy burdens on the peasant economy (through servile obligations and particularly heriot) and caused social problems (through the marriage restrictions). As the peasants could render the servile dues only from their

holdings, they imposed heavily upon the net income from agriculture. The economic burden was felt to be too heavy. Although there are almost as many complaints about landlordship as about servitude, they are less vehement. Hence there is no reason to assume a particular crisis of landlordship, but rather

2. a crisis of the agrarian economy: the extensive demands in the sphere of forest and commons, fishing and hunting suggest that there were many disquieting factors in the state of the agrarian economy, which could reach an unacceptable level even by minor increases of a new tax or the like.

3. The complaints about the judicial powers of the feudal lords were as important as the economic ones. These seigneurial rights were the ones which permitted the 'lordship' to transform into 'principality' and the yeoman (*Holden*) into 'subject'.

I

Characteristic of all Upper Swabian estates of 1525, in virtually identical form, serfdom was essentially the product of a process of intensification of lordship.[4] There is evidence that in most of the monastic estates serfdom emerged as late as 1400. Before that peasants were at least *de facto* even if not *de jure* free to move, to choose their lord and their spouses. Inconsistency of terminology also points to the relative novelty of the institution. Only in the fifteenth century did the precise terms 'bondsman' and 'serf' (*Eigenmann, Leibeigener*) displace the older, more vague and indifferentiated expressions of *Gotteshausmann* (man of the abbey), poor man, common man. The change in terminology indicates structural changes in the agrarian system that became relevant to both the legal and economic position of the peasants. In the first part of the fifteenth century, seigneurs attempted to bind 'their peasants' to themselves, regardless of their traditional status as freeholders, yeomen or tenants, by intensifying personal dependence. This restrictive policy involved the prohibition of free choice of seigneur, the prevention of free movement and the punishment of those subjects who married serfs of other lords in so-called extra-tenurial (*ungenossame*) marriages.

These commands were emphasized by the severe sanctions imposed on the trespassers: confiscation of the property of peasants who withdrew from their lord and disinheritance in case of extra-tenurial marriage. 'Flight', as the sources on the seigneurs' side called the free movement and the choice of a lord, became virtually impossible, since the common interests of all lords precluded adequate defence against a former seigneur and the economic sanctions ruined the peasant's livelihood. Extra-tenurial marriages placed a burdensome mortgage on the property. If the fines for it were not, as in the monastic estates of Rot, added to the annual dues, it meant—as in the estates of the abbeys Weingarten and Schussenried—that besides the heriot, two thirds of the man's or one third of the woman's property were confiscated by the lord, so that the children of such marriages were practically disinherited.

It is not difficult to imagine the conflicts in villages and even families, caused by the reactivation of serfdom, especially when one considers that at the beginning of the fifteenth century there were hardly any closed areas of serfdom (*Leibherrschaft*) in Upper Swabia and serfs were as scattered as were land holdings, every village containing peasants of several lords. To punish extra-tenurial marriages as severely as they did, sometimes even with the prohibition 'to partake in the Host of the holy Body of Christ', was tantamount to an inhibition of marriage. This could cause grave consequences for a small social unit such as a village and give rise to considerable aggression, since essential necessities of life had to remain unsatisfied. The thwarting of free movement could lead, under disadvantageous demographic conditions, to heavy overpopulation in the villages, which in turn caused a deterioration of the land-peasant ratio and hence a sharp differentiation between rich and poor.

Serfdom, the cause of these different tensions that led to numerous revolts in the fifteenth century and finally to the Peasant War itself was imposed unwillingly on the peasants by the feudal lords. The latter's income decreased in the course of the late medieval agrarian crisis through the fall of grain prices, their revenues in kind declined as a result of the massive migration into the cities, and finally their very seigneurial and political power tended to wane through the departure of their tenants.

The enforcement of serfdom, its intensification and extension to peasants of higher status—like *Muntleute,* copyholders and ecclesiastical tenants— had thus a double function: to preserve as far as possible the economic basis of feudal lordship and to retain its political power. This meant for the peasant as a farmer that, regardless of his earlier legal status, he now had to give the best cattle and the best cloth as heriot, that his legacy escheated to the lord if he died without offspring or left only married (i.e. endowed) children, that up to two thirds of his property was lost to his family if he married another lord's serf, which he could scarcely avoid doing in the small 'mixed' village community. For the peasant as a subject, the prohibition of free movement and free choice of a seigneur and the punishment for extra-tenurial marriage meant an increase of pressure from above. This was particularly true where, as in Upper Swabia, the lords managed to develop and sustain an exclusive claim of lordship over their subjects (this term now being really justified!), based on the combination of landlordship and serfdom. In 1448 the Abbey of Weissenau had its tenants acknowledge in an agreement that as their lord it had the right to command services, issue statutes and mete out punishment to its subjects. The peasants of the monastery of Rot had to swear in 1456 that as proprietary men (*Eigenleute*) of the abbot and the convent they shall be 'servile, subject and obedient'. The peasants of Weingarten Abbey in Hagenau had to agree in 1523 that on the basis of their servitude they acknowledge the almost absolute sovereignty of the abbey over their villages. In the Allgäu region the lords claimed unchallenged the right to tax, call to arms and judge their peasants.

The close links between lordship (*Leibherrschaft*) and magistrate (*Obrigkeit*)—more precisely, the territorial authority (*Landeshoheit*) developed from serfdom for economic and political reasons—were characteristic of most estates in Upper Swabia, although there were some where the local authority was developed from landlordship. The peasants of 1525 were well aware of the connection between serfdom and dominion. The demand for the abolition of serfdom could be and actually was understood by the lords as an attempt to dislodge the entire magistrate-subject relationship. Martin Luther, among others, saw these connections quite well, when he wrote in his *Warning for Peace to the Twelve Articles:* '. . . you are about to take the power (*gewallt*) and the right away from the magistrates, nay everything what they have. What else remains to them if the power is lost?' The reassuring words of the Twelve Articles, stating that the demands on serfdom do not intend to abolish the authority of magistrates, are to be understood in the light of the almost exclusive foundation of the latter upon the former.

II

The practice of the secular and spiritual lords, of using the institution of serfdom to confiscate their tenants' properties and exact high death duties, in order to compensate for their losses caused by the agrarian crisis, had protracted repercussions in the land tenure system. While around 1400 successful peasant farming may have led to a modest wealth which could be handed down to the next generations, these peasant fortunes were decimated by the death duties of the fifteenth century. Particularly serious—because irreversible—were the claims of the lords to a third or a half of the land because these also included the peasants' allodial holdings. Thus the peasants had to obtain their income solely from their servile holdings burdened with high rents. Weingarten Abbey appropriated through the dues an average 20 per cent of the yield, with rather uneven distribution of loads, which implied that some (mainly the smaller) units had to render up to 40 per cent of their harvest. In another monastic estate, in Heggenbach, the rent in grain was calculated on the basis of arable land and reached—apart from the tithe and dues owed to the larder—some 30 per cent of the crop. It is true, however, as D. Sabean [*1972: 21-35*] has statistically demonstrated, that rents were not substantially increased, either for tenancies which had to be renewed in every generation or for the hereditary ones. When therefore the complaints are consistent against high rents, though not claiming that they had been recently increased, then there must have been extraneous factors which made the traditional dues appear intolerable. Costumals (*urbaria*) and other manorial records of the fifteenth-sixteenth centuries suggest some of these factors. They point to a rapid increase of hired labourers and, wherever it was possible, to the expansion of arable land by forest clearing. The peasants of the Messkirch estates complained in 1525 that they 'are overcrowded by *Söldner* or wage-labourers whose extensive use of the common pasture makes it impossible for them to earn their livelihood from their farms in the usual manner'. However, the Chronicle of Zimmer reports that upon inquiry into the matter, the hired labourers proved to be the sons, sons-in-law and other relatives of the peasants. It was the increased demand for holdings, caused by population growth, which decreased the productivity of agricultural units and caused the complaints about high rents. This *argumentum ex silentio* obtains empirical proof from the rental register of Ottobeuren. Between 1480 and 1548 the population grew by 50 per cent but the average size of a family—based on a fair sample of 500 families—grew only from 5·04 to 5·60. That the total population growth is not fully reflected in greater family size suggests that the number of families increased, and this meant, assuming a constant size of available arable land, an increase of hired labourers (*Söldner*).

It was the outcome of the deterioration of land-peasant ratio and the consequent loss of income of the individual holding that additional burdens on the peasant economy acquired a much greater emphasis among the complaints than their actual significance would have warranted. The demands of the Twelve Articles regarding the supply of lumber and firewood and the restitution of hunting rights have a common cause. Lumber, the most important raw material of the Middle Ages and the early modern period, became scarce. The demand for wood by the numerous free cities of Upper Swabia drove up the price of lumber and of firewood considerably. This led first to uncontrolled cutting of the forest, but soon the need for a long term policy of conservation as the only way to avoid disaster was realized. Another incentive for better forest management came from the hunting passion of the lords secular and spiritual, as the game population naturally decreased with the rapid deforestation. Nothing was more logical than to limit the peasants' rights to exploit and use the forest, in order to secure and increase the game. Upper Swabian peasants used to acquire some additional income by burning charcoal or by selling wood; these rights were mostly lost by the late fifteenth to early sixteenth century. More injurious was the fixing or restricting of the peasants' rights to herbage and pannage. The usual portions of forest allotted to certain tenancies (*Lehenhölzer*) were often cancelled and the rights of access to the woods strictly regulated.

The peasants did not deny the need for a conservationist stance. The Twelve Articles contain the assurance that their demands will not cause the 'destruction of the woodlands', as they propose to have officers of the communities observe an orderly exploitation. However, they had no sympathy for the lords of the forest who enriched themselves at the peasants' expense; and, actually, the seigneurial income from sale of lumber was quite considerable. There was probably no Upper Swabian monastery that would not have increased its revenues in this way, and the same holds true for the nobles. The minor monastery of Gutenzell sold in one year (1562) lumber to the city of Ulm for 300 guilders. In 1554 the Fuggers sold 700 Fl. worth of beechwood to Ulm, cut in their recently acquired estate of Boos for the ridiculous sum of 29,000 Fl. The crucial importance of wood was enhanced by the fact that cities were anxious to acquire woodland, in order to become self-supporting, while the lords of land and forest also tried to extend their possession of wood. Passionate hunters as abbots and noblemen were, they wished to keep out the peasants from their game reserves. The Innsbruck government made it quite clear when writing to the forest-warden of the margraviate Burgau that beech and oak be particularly guarded, as they supply the deer and boar with fodder and shelter.

Limitation of pannage, curtailment of common meadows and increase of labourers and small-holders caused inevitably a decrease of cattle in the peasant households. Around 1500 village bye-laws began to regulate the stock. Before that date, every peasant could have as many cattle as he was able to keep through the winter. Once the access to pasture was reduced, the hay from the meadows had to be partially used up during the summer. This meant a decrease in stock, i.e. in peasant wealth.

The demand for the freedom of hunting and the waters is to be understood from this overall declining return from agrarian economy. The nobles' passion for the chase (and the complaints are almost exclusively voiced by peasants on noble estates) caused considerable harm to the fields. The limitation of peasant access to the waters not only meant curtailment of fishing, but also that of irrigation of meadows and the watering of the beasts. The abbot of Rot punished trespassers with excommunication, procured an imperial privilege for exclusive fishing rights in his entire territory and raised—with imperial approval—the fines for poaching twentyfold.

It is tempting to follow Hermann Heimpel's suggestion that the demand for freedom of hunting and fishing was actually a revolutionary symbol since venison and fish counted par excellence as seigneurial food. However, an analysis of the background of the Twelve Articles shows that the article on hunting is limited to the villages of noblemen, while the fishing complaints are rather more widespread. Internal connections between these two demands can be seen on the one hand in their economic significance—damage to the fields through the hunt and loss of foodstuff through curtailment of fishing—and in their justification by the words of Genesis, on the other, but not in any other respect.

The Twelve Articles correctly reflect Upper Swabian conditions by not including the subject of taxes as a special paragraph. There is implicit reference to it in the article about the tithe, where the 'big tithe' is to be reserved, after the payment of the pastor and the alms to the poor, for the needs of the defence of the realm. There were indeed no land taxes levied in Upper Swabia, and the only tax that some peasant households had to pay was a war-tax, called *Reissteuer*, levied for the Empire and the Swabian League. The peasants on urban and noble estates were mostly exempt from this burden. The cities paid the tax for quite a long time, well beyond 1525, from their regular budget and the nobles were still able to fulfil their obligations by staffing the castles. Thus this tax was mainly a problem of peasants on monastic estates and caused there, at any rate together with other complaints, unrest and revolt. The tenants' revolt in Rot against these taxes around 1500 was crushed by military power and the incarceration of the rebelrousers. In Ochsenhausen the rebellion was smothered by a compromise: the peasants acceded to the tax for the concession of all their holdings being made hereditary instead of renewable.

III

Growing economic burdens and, in their train, the menace to rural society drove the peasants towards a crisis of authority, which was aggravated by political developments. The decades before 1525 in Upper Swabia can be summarily characterized by the attempts of noble and monastic landlords to transform their lordship into petty states or principalities. This implied the degradation of the status of their yeomen into that of subjects (*Untertanen*). The demand of the Twelve Articles for a return to the older, positive law, without discretionary legislation (*Willkür*), has its basis in 50 per cent of the local and regional documents complaining about the legal practices of the magistracies of 1525.

In the early fifteenth century legislation, administration of justice and related matters were still to a great extent in the hands of communal-corporative bodies. The nobles and the abbots were initially rather indifferent to these matters, so that they devolved unchallenged to the communities. The numerous Upper Swabian monasteries were, as reformed abbeys, essentially devoted to their religious calling and did not care too much about their seigneurial rights, as long as the livelihood for the monks was supplied by the revenues from their endowments. The nobility of the region found its main activity in imperial service. The apparent disinterest in seigneurial rights can also be explained by the extensive jurisdiction of the imperial governors of Upper Swabia (*Reichslandvögte*), who held in their hands the administration of high justice, of forest law and of the safe conduct. This strong position of the delegate of the central authority in the fourteenth century had, of course, its origins on the central rôle of Swabia in the Hohenstaufen empire of the thirteenth. Rural society had its own institutions to handle basic 'governmental' business: to keep the peace and to mete out justice. The villages were, as a rule, administered by peasant officers with such names as wardens (*Ammänner*), judges, 'the Four', *Gemeindepfleger* [see above, document II, p. 19], etc. They took care of the difficult task of regulating the fields, the order of pastures, the irrigation of meadows, the distribution of wood-allotments; they issued, sometimes in the name of the lord, bye-laws for the life in the community and they heard and decided cases of low justice and arbitration in the village court. In the fifteenth century the competences in the administrative and legal sphere were shifted from the village community to the seigneurie. The lords began to exert pressure on the election of communal bodies and officers and finally replaced them by appointed ones. The rules and prohibitions issued by the lords were to guard the new interests of the nobles and monastic seigneurs in the village. Suddenly the common forest, the waters, the meadows, fire-fighting and the Sunday service received unprecedented attention from above. The village courts were as good as ruined by becoming nothing but administrators of seigneurial fines and punishments, losing entirely their old legislative functions. It is quite likely that social tensions, petrified oligarchies and economic crises had, by that time, made many villages into unviable political organisms. It is also possible that it was necessary, as the lords put it 'for the glory of God, the betterment and increase of the subjects and for their wealth and progress and . . . the common weal', to interfere in and regulate communal matters. But it is more probable that the cause for the growing engagement by the seigneurs lies in a change of attitude to lordship. The increasing number of village bye-laws in the fifteenth century, these written records for the growing complexity of competences, indicate the lords' new awareness of matters of administration. At the same time, the monastic estates replaced their clerical *procuratores* and stewards by secular officers. These bailiffs and wardens, mostly from urban families of the free imperial cities, devoted themselves energetically and efficiently to their administrative, policing and juridical tasks. They took care of collecting fines, controlled weights and measures, inspected mills, revised boundaries, supervised the payment of tithes and checked the accounts. Occasionally they even had special police troops at their disposal who gave appropriate weight to the seigneurial statutes, deterred rebellious peasants and arrested refractory subjects who then vanished in the jails, which we now know existed.

These administrative measures may appear petty in comparison to the early modern state, but they demonstrate a new consciousness of the Upper Swabian lords which is clearly focused on a long term aim: the territorial principality. The picture of lordship in early fifteenth century Upper Swabia was indeed very chequered. Although a concentration of manors and serfs around the centre of the estate—castle, monastery, town—can be observed, there were possessions spread far and wide into the sphere of interest of many other seigneurs. It was relatively easy to build a territory from landlordship: distant possessions could be sold and for their price others bought within the radius of interest. This process went relatively unchallenged, because apparently all lords were anxious to concentrate their holdings near the castle, the abbey or the city. If this was accompanied by the demand for submission into serfdom in return for the grant of a holding, the lord accomplished a compact area of lordship that could not be penetrated save perhaps by the wielder of high justice. While around 1400 it was typical to have three or four lords holding more or less equal amounts of land in every village, during the following century this picture changed decisively in favour of one seigneur, who—when he became the dominant landlord—was also regarded as the local magistrate (*Ortsobrigkeit*).

In other areas, like in the southern part of Upper Swabia, serfdom was the main instrument of building territorial lordship. Landlordship was not

Background of the Twelve Articles

suitable for this task, since in the area from the Lake of Constance to the River Lech jurisdiction—the right of taxation and military authority—was exclusively in the hands of the (personal) lords and not of the landlords. The Prince-Abbot of Kempten described the social legal structure of the Allgäu rather fittingly, when he based his claims thus: 'It is here namely so that the farms belong to the serfs, and the selfsame serfs belong to their lords, and each serf (*aigen man*) and his household is subject to the jurisdiction of his lord, and only to him does he owe suit of court, submission to punishment, taxes and obedience . . .' Here the territorial principality had to be built on the basis of personal dependence, on serfdom. Only through the restriction of freedom of movement and of marriage could the area be transformed. However, serfs were not to be bought and sold, and so, as an alternative, they were exchanged; first man for man, woman for woman, then groups of 10 to 20 persons, finally through contracts which transferred the ownership of more than 1,000 serfs at once. The peasant remained where he was, to farm his holding as before, only his lord had been replaced. The result was the same as in the territories where landlordship prevailed: territories were formed, in which there was only one lord, who could claim exclusive overlordship in matters of justice, taxes and defence alike.

This territorialization meant for the peasant an increased pressure from his lord in comparison to the older, more loose dependencies. Lordship over land and person, mostly also over the court, where now in one hand, while in the older structures the rivalries of the different lords left a certain vacuum and offered possibilities of manoeuvre. Now the lord was always reasonably close to his peasants, could tighten his administrative net around them and control them more efficiently. The peasants of various legal statuses, freeholders, copyholders, church-tenants and the like became uniformly subjects and the lordship was turned into dominion.

IV

The economic difficulties, the social tensions and the political pressures, discussed above, added up to a critical situation, in a form that had probably not existed ever before, ready to explode. However, one should not overlook the differences in all this uniformity. To the peasants their natural enemies and opponents appeared hierarchically ordered. The complaints against the cities were rather limited. The grievances about commons, pasture, hunting and fishing were virtually unmentioned: only in regard to herbage were there some problems. The communal administration seems to have been left intact, the tax-burden was acceptable and the differences in judicial matters were limited to certain questions of competence. The complaints against landlordship—requests rather than demands—were more numerous than those against serfdom, but remained well behind the demands of the peasants of noble and monastic estates. The peasants in the villages of nobles had grievances against the services exacted (probably boonwork for the hunt) and against the curtailment of herbage, but they altogether weighed less than the *gravamina* against the abbeys. In the monastic villages the peasants polemicized against the high rents, the heriot and entrance fee, the prohibition of extra-tenurial marriages, the inequities in the administration of justice, the interference with their rights to the waters and against the war-tax. It was therefore not only the contradiction between spiritual office and secular power that singled out the clergy as the main enemy of the peasants, but also the seriously grave conditions on ecclesiastical estates. That the actual attack hit the nobility first, suggests, however, that the tensions there were not much less.

The Twelve Articles indicate a fundamental crisis in the system of reference between peasant and lord. Feudalism of this mould became obviously petrified, unresponsive, rigid; in brief, it was unable to solve the problems otherwise than at the expense of the peasants. The peasants believed that the Twelve Articles might at least defuse this crisis. They even expected to overcome feudalism with the help of the Gospel and Divine Justice, which promised them an entirely open, fresh start for building a new society and authority.

NOTES

[1] Critical edition by Gotze [*1902*]; see also above, pp. 14-18.

[2] A number of technical terms for legal and social categories have been rendered by the best known corresponding English term, even if as in most cases they do not quite correspond with the complex usage of sixteenth century Germany. To do otherwise would have burdened the reader with innumerable circumlocutions and long foreign words. The most important expressions are given in parenthesis on the first occurrence. Apologies are offered for the imprecision caused by this simplification.—J.M.B.

[3] These have been printed by Franz [*1935: nos. 24, 26, 28, 30-31; 1963: nos. 28, 34-36, 40, 56*], by Baumann [*1877: nos. 58, 62, 104, 133*] and by Vogt [*1879-83: nos. 34, 47, 55, 59, 67c, 880, 882-83, 885-87, 890-92, 895, 898a, 900 and 903*].

[4] The following arguments are based, besides the primary material quoted above (n. 3) on my studies [*Blickle 1972, 1973, 1975a, and 1975*], and other monographs, e.g., Baumann [*1883-4*], Gruber [*1956*], Maurer [*1973*], Nuber [*1961*], Saarbrücker Arbeitsgruppe [*1974*]. References to single points have been omitted.

REFERENCES

Baumann, F. L., 1877, *Akten zur Geschichte des deutschen Baernkrieges aus Oberschwaben.*
Baumann, F. L., 1883-94, *Geschichte des Allgäus*, 3 vols. (repr. 1971-73).
Baumann, F. L., 1896, *Die Zwölf Artikel des oberschwäbischen Baurn 1525.*
Blickle, P., 1972, Bauer und Staat in Oberschwaben, *Zeitschrift fur wurttembergische Landesgeschichte* 31, 104-120.
Blickle, P., 1973, *Landschaften im Alten Reich. Die staatliche Funktion des gemeinen Mannes in Oberdeutschland.*
Blickle, P., 1975, 'Agrarkrise und Leibeigenschaft im spätmittelalterlichen deutschen Südwesten, *Reagrarisierung und ländliches Nebengewerbe im Spätmittelalter und im 19. Jahrhundert*, ed. H. Kellenbenz.

Blickle, P., 1975, *Die Revolution von 1525*.
Franz, G., 1935, *Der deutsche Bauernkrieg. Aktenband* (repr. 1968).
Franz, G., 1939, Die Entstehung der 'Zwölf Artikel der deutschen Bauernschaft', *Archiv für Reformationsgeschichte*, 36, 195–213.
Franz, G., 1963, *Quellen zur Geschichte des Bauernkrieges*.
Gotze, A., 1902, 'Die zwölf Artikel der Bauern 1525', *Historische Vierteljahrschrift*, 5, 1–33.
Gruber, E., 1956, *Geschichte des Klosters Ochsenhausen*. Tübingen Thesis Ph.D.
Nipperdey, Th.-P. Melcher, 1966, 'Bauernkrieg', *Sowjetsystem und Demokratische Gesellschaft*, ed. C. D. Kernig, 1: 611–627.
Nuber, W., 1961, *Studien zur Besitz- und Rechtsgeschichte des Klosters Rot von seinen Anfängen bis 1618*, Tübingen Thesis Ph.D.
Maurer, H.-M., 1973, 'Die Ausbildung der Territorialgewalt oberschwabischer Kolster vom 14. bis zum 17. Jahrhundert', *Blätter für deutsche Landesgeschichte*, 109, 151–195.
Sabean, D. W., 1972, *Landbesitz und Gesellschaft am Vorabend des Bauernkrieges*.
Saarbrücker Arbeitsgruppe, 1974, 'Die spätmittelalterliche Leibeigenschaft in Oberschwaben', *Zeitschrift für Agrargeschichte und Agrarsoziologie*, 22, 9–23.
Vogler, G., 1975, 'Der revolutionäre Gehalt und die räumliche Verbreitung der Zwölf Artikel', *Revolte und Revolution in Europa*, ed. P. Blickle (Historische Zeitschrift, Sonderheft 4).
Vogt, W., 1879–1883, 'Die Correspondenz des schwäbischen Bundeshauptmannes Ulrich Artzt von Augsburg aus den Jahre 1524–1527. Ein Beitrag zur Geschichte des Schwäbischen Bundes und des Bauernkrieges', *Zeitschrift des Historischen Vereins für Schwaben und Neuburg*, 6, 7, 9, 10.
Walder, E., 1954, 'Der politische Gehalt der Zwölf Artikel der deutschen Bauernschaft von 1525', *Schweizer Beiträge zur allgemeinen Geschichte* 12, 5–22.

German Agrarian Institutions at the Beginning of the Sixteenth Century: Upper Swabia as an Example

David Sabean[*]

This paper deals with three dynamic factors leading to rural social change in the years before 1525. The rise of population changed man/land ratios, brought alterations in inheritance customs, and helped create a class of landless agricultural labourers. Alterations in the nature of market relationships changed the balance between city and country and introduced new wage relationships in the countryside with the putting out system. Increasing articulation of state institutions led to attempts to rationalise armed force, brought taxation to pay for larger and more complex armies, and changed the relationships between central authority and subjects. The effects of these changes should be investigated regionally before generalisations about all of Central Europe are made, and the paper shows how one such regional study might be done.

Historical research on Central Europe dealing with the peasantry or with peasant political activity has not been sufficiently concerned with sociological questions. It has been assumed that the degree of rural social differentiation either has not been great or has been of insufficient interest for analysing particular problems at hand. The research that has been done has tended to confine itself either to questions relating to legal categories [*Seldner, Köppler, Vollbauer*, etc.] or to gross measures of stratification such as frequency distributions of land holding. We know, for example, very little about such questions as how the internal working of the farm-tenant families differed from those of day labourers.

Nowhere is this approach clearer than in research devoted to the Peasant War—Marxist and non-Marxist alike. Smirin [1956 : 492, 497 ff], for example, penetrates no further into the society than to mention that the area around Memmingen was important for wheat cultivation. Franz [1965 : 22] mentions that the Remstal was particularly heavily populated because of the effects of viniculture but makes no more of the fact. Nowhere does an historian systematically explore regional differences in population density, mobility, village structure, social stratification, or integration into the market in

[*] *University of Pittsburgh. This article was presented to the Memmingen Conference, held earlier in 1975, and has been published with the rest of the proceedings in 'Revolte und Revolution in Europa', Historische Zeitschrift, Beiheft 4, 1975. It is printed here by kind permission of P. Blickle, editor and Oldenbourg Verlag, Munich.*

order to explore uniformities and contrasts in political activity. Part of the reason for the neglect no doubt has been because the best research has been done on political programmes which do not seem to be the result of such differences.[1] Even Engels who gives the most detailed analysis of interest groups in German society at the beginning of the sixteenth century, relating class interests to ideological positions, confines himself to the grossest generalizations about differences within rural society. Working within Engels' tradition East German historiography has on occasion begun a more sophisticated analysis [*Loesche, 1961*].

The question boils down to whether in peasant uprisings or other protests against outsiders villagers act with solidarity or whether well articulated interest groups within the village press for different ends or indeed whether differences cancel themselves out, inhibiting revolt. Not all groups in rural society are equally capable of articulation of interests or in expressing themselves in political activity.

To some degree the question of rural social articulation is governed by the degree to which rural society is integrated into the market. A particularly good example of the problem is afforded by the analysis of Russian society at the end of the nineteenth and beginning of the twentieth century. Working with a model based on Western European experience, Russian observers expected class differences to be translated into political consciousness within village society. A recent systematic comparison of each Russian province in its participation in the fourth Duma fails to find any differences in political activity between different classes of peasants from Kulak to the poorest member of the rural community in most of the Russian regions [*Vinogradoff, 1974*]. The conclusion is that for most of Russia the market was hardly existent and that therefore politically conscious differences failed to arise. In the Baltic provinces, however, rural society was fully integrated into the market, which led to the transformation of agricultural structure and the articulation of clear social differences and consequent political ideology and activity [*ibid. 129-194*].

While agriculture was oriented towards the market by the early sixteenth century in Central Europe, the degree to which regional variations existed is not generally clear from the literature, nor is it clear to what degree village social differences were articulated and conscious to village members. As a consequence of a rising population, the sixteenth century saw increased specialization based on market exchange—one thinks immediately of viniculture, dairying, and rural textile production. To what degree these changes wrought significant sociological differences needs to be investigated.

This paper does not attempt to do what the author would like to see done—that is to survey regional differences in social structure and market orientation. Rather the purpose is to raise questions from an intense analysis of one region which participated in the Peasant War so as to provoke discussion from those whose specializations afford far more expertise on other regions than the author [*Sabean, 1972*] is able to muster.

In carrying out this task the paper will be concerned with various institutions that express themselves at the village level. In doing so we will deal with certain structural problems and change effected by population, the market, and the state. The treatment will be rather uneven, with greater attention given to the first of these considerations. It is important at the outset to be clear about the way the problems are posed. The early sixteenth century was a period of population rise for Central Europe, but the question most simply put is not whether and to what extent population rose. For systematic and comparative analysis the proper question is related to the balance between population and resources at the village level. How are the balance of population and changes in its level expressed in the structure of social relationships? It is not enough, when one speaks of the market, to allude to increased monetarization of peasant economic activity or to refer generally to increased penetration of market relationships. The issue is to analyse exactly in what way changes in relationship to the market affects any particular peasant and how the experiences of different rural groups vary. Do these changes bring about consequent changes in attitudes or social relations between various rural groups? How do regions vary in response to change, for example, bocage vs. open fields, hilly vs. plains, dairying vs. viniculture, grain vs. market gardening, agricultural vs. rural industrial.

With regards to the state it is likewise not enough to compare directly different institutions such as *Leibeigenschaft*. This is a common error most recently evidenced in Gerlach's [*1974*] comparison of the Bauernkrieg with the 1381 peasant uprising in England. The fact that the peasant programmes in both uprisings inveighed against 'unfree' relationships, led the author to confuse different institutions—such as English serfdom, South German *Leibeigenschaft*, and different forms of personal bondage in other parts of Germany. The central sociological question is a broader one relating to the degree of penetration of the state into the village, how this is institutionalized, and how it affects social relationships inside the village.

Perhaps it would be well to pause here to detail the history of a 'typical' but nonexistent Wuerttemberg village during the early modern period as it relates to only one of the problem areas we have outlined—population— in order to illustrate the kind of issue that we wish to raise here, in this case the question of the social affects of changing population levels. This 'history' given here is based on scattered pieces of evidence and is subject to extensive revision in the future.[2]

A doubling of the population in a village between 1490 and 1560 would be well within expectations, so that a village of 500 people would have expanded to ca. 1,000. Between 1560 and 1620 a village would show a longterm stability in its population level, the mechanism being a periodic gouging effect of famine and epidemic disease. During the period it would not be unusual for a village of 1,000 to lose on at least three occasions 100-300 people in brief periods of exaggerated mortality. Fertility, however, remained high, causing the population to spring back to its previous level. It appears then that the rise in population found its level by the 1560s, striking a balance between population and resourses. Although Wuerttemberg appeared in the eighteenth century and even now as an area of extreme fragmentation of agricultural land, it does not seem that such great fragmentation took place in the sixteenth century. Rather a dependent group of landless labourers arose, with villages displaying great differences in wealth and in the distribution of land. The inception of a violent fluctuation in population levels does not seem to have affected this social differentiation.

The effects of the Thirty Years' War altered the structure, reducing a village of 1,000 to as low as 400. Recovery was slow since taxes were high, peasants were heavily indebted, domestic animal herds had been decimated, fields left uncultivated, buildings destroyed, and seed in short supply. Many peasants simply refused to take on inheritances, while many who wanted land could obtain it. The result in the first generation was to develop a relatively undifferentiated group of farm tenants on small properties. Successive generations partitioned each inheritance, so that by 1720 when the pre-war population level of ca. 1,000 was re-established, a completely different distribution of land and wealth had taken place. Between 1720 and 1760 the population tended to rise only very slightly, the mechanism of this stability being apparently on the fertility side. Between 1760 and 1800 the population could come close to doubling.

There are a number of lessons here that need to be stressed. A person born into this village in 1520 or 1570, 1660 or 1750 would face radically different societies simply in regards to the way population densities were related to the means of production. Population density is only one issue; one must also consider the rates of change and the mechanisms of change. The rules of succession to property, the division of labour, and mechanisms of social control are crucial institutions that channel forces of change into new sets of social relationships. How these social relationships find political expression either within the village or external to it is one of the issues that should concern the historian dealing with peasant uprisings.

Given this example and its consequent expectations it is disappointing to turn to the mass of data from the Peasant War because at first glance the differences that one expects do not seem to be evidenced in the data. The political demands of the peasants seldom reveal much about village structure or power relationships in rural society. If conflict existed in the countryside it is seldom brought to the forefront of peasant consciousness. In order to penetrate to the social reality behind peasant demands the historian must deal intensively with small regions to understand the extremely complex set of social relations and institutions. He has to imagine or reconstruct what the local effects of a set of demands would be.

A good example here is the notion of the *Gemeinde* which is so central to the Twelve Articles and emerges in other areas as well [*Sabean, 1972 : 100 ff; Buszello, 1969 : 16 ff*]. To say that the *Gemeinde* should run the common land (*Allmende*) when only a few farm tenants are enfranchised is quite different from saying the same thing where most household heads take part in decision-making in a village. The *Gemeinde* would have quite different meaning in an area of scattered farms with heavy out-migration on non-landholding population from one with nucleated settlements with a large dependent class of cottagers and landless labourers.

In Upper Swabia the movement for *Gemeinde* independence had become strong during the period of low population density and consequent reorganization of manorial economy following the Black Death. Bader [*1962* : *2, 37-85*] has shown the day to day pressure brought by villagers to take over the administration of their internal affairs and to punish offenders and settle local disputes. Since the lords had withdrawn from the economy of the village except to skim off a surplus in the form of rents, tithes, and minor services, this movement had considerable success. However, its effect was quite different in 1520 than 1420. For one thing by 1520 population densities had already altered considerably and a good deal of social differentiation had taken place. This is clear in the Twelve Articles (Article 8, above, p. 17) where the bitter complaint of tenant farmers against the alienation of common land for the landless to build cottages is expressed [*Sabean, 1972 : 44, 83, 104*].

One of the clearest examples of conflict between the two groups comes from Ochsenhausen which had an early revolt in 1502 settled by a treaty between the tenants and the abbot [*ibid., 42 ff*]. In 1502 the tenant farmers obtained the right to hereditary tenures and the right to sell their farms so long as they were not split up. This latter point was clearly in their interests and in fact was part of their negotiating terms. Farm tenants as well as the abbot desired a society in which the number of farms were not increased and so the economic viability of each farm would continue. On the other hand the abbot had alienated some of the common land of the villages giving it out to landless peasants. Such practices were opposed by the tenants, and it was written into the treaty that they should cease.

In the Ochsenhausen articles of 1525 the landless group had increased to a size large enough to dominate the demands. Article 7 demands that all land be subject to piecemeal sale. Article 15 demanded the extension of the use of common land to all inhabitants of the village. Article 16 called for the extension of the use of wood and water to the *Handwerker* (craftsmen). That the treaty of 1502 and 1525 reflected the interests of different groups is made clear in article 9 which called for the setting aside of that of 1502, 'weil er ihnen unleidenlich und nachtheilich ist und zu verderblichem Schaden gereicht' (because it is inequitable and disadvantageous to them and causes destructive damage).

As far as I know this is the only clear example from Upper Swabia in the 1525 revolt where the interests of any group outside of the tenant farmers was articulated. It is safe to say that the Twelve Articles was the programme of the tenant farmers, that is enfranchised members, those with proper *Hofstätte,* of the villages. They alone would control access to woods, fish ponds, and streams. They would appoint the priest, pay him from the tithe, and administer the rest to aid the village poor. They would select the village officials and man the village courts. No common land would be alienated for the growing class of landless and presumably the latter would be excluded from any share in the *Allmende*.

Only once was the *Gemeinde* movement specifically noted as an internal village conflict. The Zimmern Chronicle made this point, arguing that the peasants held no real dispute with their lord; rather their concern was with the landless labourers who were agitating for access to common rights. The dispute was made the more poignant because the tenant farmers and farm labourers were related to each other by blood [*see above, p. 69*].

The point of all this is to argue that social differentiation had clearly taken place by 1525 and consequent conflict over the division of resources was part of the revolt. Apart from the statements in the Ochsenhausen articles and the short passage in the Zimmern Chronicle it would be easy to read all the rest of the chronicles and the articles of grievance and to miss this aspect. It would be natural to conclude that the '*Gemeinde*' of 1525 was the same thing as that of 1425, that political consciousness was that of closed, unified villages gradually extending their competence vis-à-vis their lords. The questions to be opened for discussion here are: what was the regional distribution of the *Gemeinde* movement in 1525? Where was it central, where peripheral, where non-existent? What were the different social contexts in which it was articulated? If it were successful in any region who would gain, who suffer?

Now it is necessary to turn to a more systematic examination of the three forces of change affecting institutions and agriculture, first the rise of population which in Upper Swabia became important from 1450 onwards. Annual growth rates of 1-1·5 per cent are quite possible for the region, which would mean at least a doubling of the population in 70 years.

In a period of rising population each village was faced with the problem of dividing resources among more people. It should be remembered that 'land' is not a static concept, for it can be worked with more or less intensity depending among other things on the number of people to work it. Under certain conditions a rise in population simply results in a similar rise in production. In Upper Swabia there is evidence of renewed clearing, but at some point late in the fifteenth century expansion of the arable could be done only at the expense of existing farms, by dividing the *Allmende*.

The mechanism which allocates rights to property and access to village resources is in the first place the rules of inheritance. Where all children of a family are treated equally under conditions of growing population increased social differentiation takes place as a matter of course, since families vary in size. Le Roy Ladurie [*1966 : 1, 237 ff*] has given a good example of the process for Languedoc in the sixteenth century. But in this as in everything else regions react quite differently. It is not enough to compare regions of partible inheritance with those of impartible, for legal requirements are constantly twisted according to peasant requirements.

In Upper Swabia as a result of population pressure a series of changes in inheritance rules took place. There were two basically different reactions associated respectively with the city of Ravensburg and the abbey of Weingarten. Ravensburg let out its farms as inheritable tenancies at the beginning of the fifteenth century [Sabean, 1972 : 22 f, 40 ff]. As population rose the city first fought demands to split up farms among the heirs, but by the 1480s the movement was in full swing. As farms fractionalized the city purchased the portions from the heirs, reunifying them and letting them out as life-time leases to only one person. Thus the century saw a movement away from a structure where all siblings shared equally in the inheritance as long as they stayed on the farm. Low population density allowed a farm to maintain a balance between its population and resources. Extra young people could leave to go to other, underpopulated farms as spouses or for a time as servants or farm labourers. As population densities increased greater competition forced farms to accommodate more people and brought pressure to break them up. The result of the city's policies was to maintain the farms as a constant number and to ensure that only one child would take over the farm in each generation. This effectively meant that the remaining siblings were sharply differentiated from the heir and were reduced to the permanent status of farm labourers or servants.

Weingarten Abbey's history is slightly different [Sabean, 1972 : 21]. Between 1440 and 1470 farms were leased for the lifetime of a married couple and all of their children, reflecting the conditions of relatively low population density. Between 1470 and 1540 leases were for the lifetime of the couple and their youngest son. This effectively worked the same as in the Ravensburg case, radically differentiating between the heir and the other siblings. After 1540 leases were for the lifetime of a married couple only.

These two are an instructive example of different forms of land tenure and inheritance rules existing in close proximity. They both reacted to the same pressures in ways that fulfilled the logic of the institutions themselves and the pressure they underwent. Although the rules at both ends of the process were different as were the paths they took in going from one condition to the other, the upshot was the same—care for an entire family throughout its lifetime by the home farm with relative maintenance of status of all siblings at the beginning of the process and radical differentiation of status for the adult siblings at the end.

The way these changes affected the family is important. Relations within the family and the nature of the domestic unit are among the least researched questions relating to German rural society. Le Roy Ladurie [1966 : 1, 160ff] has demonstrated how population pressure brought to an end the extended family characteristic of parts of Languedoc in the fifteenth century. Perhaps such an extended family existed in early fifteenth-century Upper Swabia. Pulverization of land made large family units unnecessary and impractical in Languedoc. The threat of pulverization or overpopulation on farms also reinforced the nuclear family in Upper Swabia, even though farms often remained large enough to need labour from outside the family.

With the stress on the nuclear family of mother, father, and dependent children came the process of radical social differentiation among the sibling group once it attained adulthood. The effects of this kind of social structure can have quite different implications depending upon the region involved. Where rural weaving became important, children might be attracted by the possibility of moving out relatively early, marrying, and becoming independent [*Mendels, 1970*]. In other regions the attraction of a city or frontier might siphon off the excess population. Where a region maintained primary dependence on agriculture, however, and mobility played a minor role, a family could have quite fierce competition for succession within its ranks. There are cases in Europe where the son who has no hope for inheritance developed an 'entrepreneurial' spirit [*Kasden, 1965*]. In other instances the prospect of not receiving the land is debilitating and develops a spirit of dependence [*Authenrieth, 1779 : 40*].

In Upper Swabia at the beginning of the sixteenth century the region was still in a process of rapid change, and it is to be expected in such circumstances that the family would develop unusual tensions. Earlier in the fifteenth century primary links were probably those between first-degree kin, parents and siblings. Younger children probably in fact often succeeded to farms since older children, reaching their majority and wishing to marry and become independent, could go elsewhere, the sons, e.g., marrying into farms where only daughters survived. The pressure to remain at home that developed later in the century gave the advantage to elder sons who could lay claim to rights earlier than the younger children. The prospect of winning all or losing all must have created unusual tensions in the family, the experience of each succeeding generation being different from the former. By the early sixteenth century primary links between siblings were being de-emphasized (the Messkirch example) as tenant farmers closed their ranks together. A good modern example of this has been discussed for lower Austria by Sigrid Kehera [*1972*], where the same kind of radical social differentiation among siblings took place. Adult siblings avoided each other except for a formal bow at the church door on Sunday mornings. Farm tenants developed associations (e.g., *the Stammtisch*) among themselves that excluded their siblings.

Another important issue that needs to be discussed relates to the fabric of village relations, especially with regards to the use of common land. It is a common practice among historians to view the peasants as a conservative force. With population, the market, and the state constantly altering conditions, the peasantry is seen as fighting a rearguard action. This is not the whole picture, as the *Gemeinde* movement in South Germany shows. Still, as we have seen, 1525 is not simply the high point in this movement of village self control. In the early fifteenth century the *Gemeinde* movement implied a conflict between lord and villager. In 1525 it was more of a three way tangle between lord, tenant farmer, and labourer or cottager. The question of who had rights in the village and how they were to be parcelled out and regulated was a dominant one. The dispute was expressed in *Gemeinde* movement ideology because the village corporation was by this time so strong and was used to accommodate new pressures. Tenant farmers resented lords interfering either to protect a portion of the population or to extend the latter's own income by allocating village resources unilaterally to those not enjoying such rights [*Sabean, 1972 : 44, 83, 104*].

So far we have dealt with the effects of population rise in increasing social differentiation. It also helped to exacerbate the economic tensions. An increased population puts greater pressure on the demand for foodstuffs, particularly grain, and increases the labour supply. It also helps through the price mechanism to increase regional specialization—sheep raising in the Thüringer Wald and wine in the Remstal. Looking at the problem from the point of view of real wages—the exchange rate between wages and wheat— over the long term before 1525 there was little change; the radical downswing came only in the 1530s [*ibid., 76 ff*]. What does take place is an increase in the rate and severity of short term fluctuations. In a period of bad harvest prices are driven much higher than before and real wages plummet. In the 25 years before the Peasant War there were two such severe periods. Since the issues between labourers and tenants were becoming so great in the period, this must have exacerbated the tensions. For a large producer (many of the farmers in Upper Swabia regularly produced a marketable surplus) a short harvest is not necessarily a bad thing: his labour needs are less and the cost of what labour he requires is much less. The offsetting rise in prices makes it possible for him to reap an extra profit. This in turn allows him to lend money and goods to the small farmer or landless labourer, collecting the debts in the subsequent period. Fluctuations by their very nature create a situation where the well-off individual can profit from the problems of the less well off.

Another issue that needs to be explored more closely is the changing balance between city and country. Since grain prices were rising and prices fluctuating more (note that the prices of industrial goods were not subject to the same fluctuations), cities were increasingly concerned with supplying themselves with a regular grain supply at steady prices in order to dampen social tensions within the walls. Perhaps some of the tension between town and village in Wüerttemberg was generated by this problem. Another region where it seems to have played a rôle is the Thüringer Wald.

Changes brought by the market are much more difficult to deal with; a thorough analysis of regional differences is not yet possible. First there is the change in relations of supply and demand stimulated by population rise. Pressure on foodstuffs is expressed primarily in grain prices. Rising demand aids in increasing regional specialization which in turn increases the rate of trade and thus creates more demand for silver. There was an increasing demand for mining products and textiles, especially for linens and fustians (*Barchent*). Profits in trading, mining, and textiles increased bourgeois wealth which in turn could be ploughed back into enterprise [*Steinmüller, 1961*]. Some of the articles of grievance from the Thüringer Wald complained about the activity of urban entrepreneurs associated with the *Verlagssystem* [*Fuchs, 1964 : 141*]. Often bourgeois wealth was invested in land so that a part of peasant land was held in tenancy from city dwellers [*Loesche, 1961*].

The chief aspect investigated here are changes brought about in rural textiles, which have a direct bearing on village social structure. Weaving became an occupation of households that could not subsist purely on agriculture. It is hard to get data on the exact social effects in the early sixteenth century, but from studies done for the seventeenth and eighteenth centuries [Mendels, 1970; Levine, 1974], there is the suggestion that dependence on weaving has a direct effect on marriage age and population structure. All over Western Europe where traditional patterns of agriculture or urban handicraft prevailed, marriages of both men and women were considerably delayed [Hajnal, 1965]. The man waited until his inheritance was available or until he could afford to set up a proper household. The woman had to wait until a dowry was forthcoming. In general the average age of marriage for men was ca. 26 and for women ca. 24, but there are examples where first marriages took place at much later ages [Wrigley, 1966]. The effects of rural textile manufacturing, in many areas, freed people from the land/marriage pattern. It allowed for earlier independence and thus earlier marriage. With early marriages came increased fertility and a shortened period between generations, so that regions associated with rural weaving also showed faster increases in population. The ultimate result was to create a population with lower per capita incomes subject to the vagaries of demand in regions far removed from the centres of production. For the eighteenth century one thinks of Silesia, Flanders and the English Midlands. In Saxony regional development displayed a pattern of traditional agricultural production, with single son inheritance, stable population, and outmigration, coupled with areas of population rise, rural industry and land fragmentation [Blaschke, 1967].

This rural textile production seems to go with new marriage patterns, an acceleration in population increase, greater rural poverty, agricultural intensification, greater social differentiation, and land fragmentation for at least a part of the population. Such regions often came to be dependent on the importation of grain, so that the population was subject to vagaries in the demand for their product and in the supply of their necessities. All of this it seems to me was only at the beginning stages by 1525, but already was affecting some regions.

In Upper Swabia the data is hard to come by. Rural weaving had been important as a part-time occupation around Ravensburg in the late fifteenth century [Sabean, 1972 : 39]. But as Ravensburg's part in the long distance trade declined, so apparently did the demand for locally produced cloth. In some areas of Upper Swabia, however, rural weaving did develop significantly [Mottek, 1968 : 189, 210].

What rôle did weavers play in the Bauernkrieg? Returning once more to the Ochsenhausen Articles, *Handwerker* are expressly mentioned in Article 16. One suspects that many of the farm labourers or cottagers who were behind the articles did some weaving. For the rest the character of the Upper Swabian revolt as being in the interests of farm tenants suggests that rural weavers may not have supported it. One more piece of evidence is important to note. In Lotzer's sketch for a *Bundesordnung* it was assumed that rural

Handwerksleute would not be part of the union [Sabean, 1972 : 12]. It was suggested that their interests did not coincide with those of the rebels.

This then is my suggestion. Rural weaving, particularly of fustians, became important in Upper Swabia by the fifteenth century and was increasing in importance. A large part of the population which had no land or only small plots were engaged in the *Verlagssystem*. These were the same people who put on pressure to divide land, to get part of the commons, to build cottages, and to take part in the use of the *Allmende*. If they acted as other rural weavers acted later, they married young, aiding the population rise, and became increasingly impoverished. In considering these issues discussion might well focus on the regional effects of market changes associated with specialization in agriculture, textile production, and mining. How was the social structure affected—density of population, the division of resources, the structure of the household and family, mobility, and the relations between city and country? To what degree did growing capitalist production affect rural social relations? Important here is the regional spread of the *Verlagssystem* and the investment of capitalist wealth into further production, consumption, or land.

The last question to be taken up is the rôle of the state in effecting change in peasant institutions and political consciousness. For Upper Swabia the chief issue was *Leibeigenschaft*. It is not necessary to discuss this institution in detail since this has been done by Blickle [*1973 : 318 ff; 1974*] (see also above, 71-73). Suffice it to say *Leibeigenschaft* played an important rôle in the cross-cutting jurisdictions in the territory. Weingarten claimed the right to tax all of its *Leibeigene*, entering into disputes with a number of neighbours on the issue [Sabean, 1972 : 95 ff]. Überlingen for one argued that taxation was based on the *Vogtrecht* or arose out of lower justice.

Briefly, it can be argued that much of the dynamism of the early modern state stemmed from the changing character of warfare and the needs of the state in maintaining internal order and waging external warfare. Widening the tax base was crucial as was the clear definition of those subject to taxation. Much of the interest in drawing boundary lines, untangling jurisdictions, and standardizing peasant inheritance rules and property rights stemmed from the interests of higher authorities in increasing taxes and in participating in warfare of various kinds. For territories such as Weingarten, *Leibeigenschaft* was important as an instrument of this policy. Much of the peasant participation in representative institutions in Southern Germany (as Blickle [*1974 : 435, 487*] has shown) revolved around the question of military obligations and taxation. The wider question to be posed then is not where *Leibeigenschaft* existed and how heavy its financial burdens were or whether peasants felt demeaned by its status. It is rather the systematic problem of how various regions were affected by the new tax demands of the state and by the attempts of the state to rationalize and standardize the conditions of the subjects. What were the variations in the tax burdens of various regions? Did different kinds of taxes affect rural society in different ways. What place did state exactions take in the entire extraction process of the peasant surplus?

With regards to *Leibeigenschaft* for Upper Swabia there are a number of ways that peasant institutions and agriculture were affected (see above 66-68). One important possible effect of increased taxation was to stimulate monetarization of the peasant enterprise, which in turn meant greater rationalization and increased production [*Tilly, 1973 : 1-10; Ardant, 1965*]. *Leibeigenschaft* being a personal form of bondage often posed a principle contrary to village self-jurisdiction. Where several lords had *Leibeigene* in the same village, they laid conflicting claims to jurisdiction, this precisely at a time when tenant farmers were stressing ties of neighbourhood [*Sabean, 1972 : 86, 100, 116*].

Paradoxically the issue of taxation was one of the few that turned peasants outwards from their villages in a common issue over any extended period of time [*Blickle, 1974 : 487 ff*]. For Upper Swabia it might be argued that within the village the direction of movement was from kin to class over the issue of participation in the *Gemeinde*. Viewed from outside the village at the same time the tendency was from village isolation to 'peasant *estate*' over the issue of taxation. Still in Upper Swabia this latter movement was only a tendency and it is important to distinguish between articulation of demands by the peasants themselves and by those leaders in the Peasant War who came from outside the peasantry [*Sabean, 1972 : 109*].

This paper has been a plea for a more sociological analysis of the German peasantry. Historians need to concern themselves with systematic, comparative questions relating to population structure, the nature of the family and the structure of kinship relations, village stratification, social control, the nature of dependence, mobility, and the articulation of the village within the wider society. It is not my purpose to press for the primacy of economic or social relationships, but only to argue that political and ideological consciousness is molded by a complex set of social relationships which in turn are closely dependent on ecological and economic factors. By and large I have neglected the aristocracy in this discussion—not a trivial omission—in order to emphasize that not all important conflict in rural society was between lord and peasant. The understanding of Central European rural society in the context of its economic, political, and institutional structure is a wide-open field for research.

NOTES

[1] Horst Buszello *1969* finds differences in political ideology a function of the kind of state structure of any particular region.

[2] I am presently working on a history of the Württemberg village of Neckarhausen. A useful book is Paul Sauer *1972: 32ff*. I have consulted the Kirchenbücher for Neckarhausen and numerous sources on population levels from the sixteenth to the eighteenth century in the Hauptstaatsarchiv Stuttgart.

REFERENCES

Ardant, Gabriel, 1965, *Théorie sociologique de l'impôt*, 2 vols., Paris.
Autenreith, J. F., 1779, *Die Uneingeschränkte Vertrennung der Bauerngüter oder Bauern-Lehen*, Stuttgart.
Bader, Karl S., 1962, *Studien zur Rechtsgeschichte der mittelalterlichen Dorfes*, II, Köln.
Blaschke, Karl Heinz, 1967, *Bevölkerungsgeschichte von Sachsen bis zur industriellen Revolution*, Weimar.
Blickle, Peter, 1973, *Landschaften im Alten Reich*, Munich.
Blickle, Peter et al., 1974, 'Die spätmittelalterliche Leibeigenschaft in Oberschwaben', *Zeitschrift für Agrargeschichte und Agrarsoziologie*, XXII.
Buszello, Horst, 1969, *Der Deutsche Bauernkrieg als Politische Bewegung*, Berlin.
Franz, Günther, 1965, *Der deutsche Bauernkrieg*, Darmstadt.
Fuchs, Walter P., ed., 1964, *Akten zur Geschichte des Bauernkriegs in Mitteldeutschland*, vol. 2, Neudruck, Aalen.
Gerlach, Horst, 1969, *Der englische Bauernaufstand von 1381 und der deutsche Bauernkrieg: Ein Vergleich*, Meisenheim am Glan.
Hajnal, J., 1965, 'European Marriage Patterns in Perspective' in D. V. Glass and D. E. C. Eversley, eds., *Population in History*, London.
Kasden, Leonard, 1965, 'Family Structure, Migration and the Entrepreneur', *Comparative Studies in History and Society*, VII.
Khera, Sigrid, 1972, 'An Austrian Peasant Village under Rural Industrialization', *Behaviour Science Notes*, VII.
Le Roy Ladurie, Emmanuel, 1966, *Les Paysans de Languedoc*, vol. 1, Paris.
Levine, David, 1974, 'The Demographic Implication of Rural Industrialization: A Family Reconstitution Study of Two Leicestershire Villages, 1600–1851', Cambridge University: dissertation.
Loesche, Dietrich, 1961, 'Zur Lage der Bauern im Gebiet der ehemaligen freien Reichstadt Mühlhausen i. Th. zur Zeit des Bauernkriegs' in Gerhard Brendler, ed., *Die Frühbürgerliche Revolution in Deutschland*, Berlin.
Mendels, Franklin, 1970, 'Industrialization and Population Pressure in Eighteenth Century Flanders', University of Wisconsin: dissertation.
Mottek, Hans, 1968, *Wirtschaftsgeschichte Deutschlands*, Berlin.
Sabean, David, 1972, *Landbesitz und Gesellschaft am Vorabend des Bauernkrieges*, Stuttgart.
Sauer, Paul, 1972, *Affalterbach 972–1972*, Affalterbach.
Smirin, M. M., 1956, *Die Volksreformation des Thomas Müntzer und der grosse Bauernkrieg*, Berlin.
Steinmüller, Karl, 1961, 'Zur Lage der Zwickauer Tuchmacherei zwischen 1470 und 1530' in Brendler, ed., *Die frühbürgerliche Revolution in Deutschland*, Berlin.
Tilly, Charles, 1973, 'Food Supply and State-Making in Europe', *Peasant Studies Newsletter*, II: 3.
Vinogradoff, Eugene D., 1974, 'The Russian Peasantry and the Electors to the Fourth Duma', Columbia University: dissertation.
Wrigley, E. A., 1966, 'Family Limitation in Pre-Industrial England', *Economic History Review*, second series, XIX.

'The Peasant War in Germany' by Friedrich Engels—125 years after

Janos Bak*

The 450th anniversary of the Peasant War was also the 125th of the publication of *The Peasant War in Germany* by Friedrich Engels. Originally a series of articles in the May-October issue of the *Neue Rheinische Zeitung* edited by Marx and Engels, *The Peasant War* was re-published in 1870 and 1875 and many times since, with prefaces by Engels. The subject remained dear to Engels for the rest of his life and was to serve as a basis for further work on the peasantry and the agrarian question. Numerous references in his correspondence and a whole series of notes testify to the plans Engels had for a more elaborate study. Shortly before his death he still counted on starting work soon: 'If only I were already at it', he wrote on May 21, 1895 [Engels, 1956 : 209].

The double anniversary suggested the idea of a discussion on the merits and significance of Engels' book, but there are many reasons that may justify such an exchange of ideas. *The Peasant War in Germany* was one of the earliest historical studies based on the philosophy and methodology elaborated by Marx and Engels. As such, it is not only a classic example of the application of the principles of social science analysis to a particular epoch but also an important piece of evidence for the development of dialectical and historical materialism itself. Engels' contribution to this development has recently been summarized as having emphasized the 'empirical and pragmatic bearing of the doctrine' [L. Krieger in *Engels* 1967 : xvii]. The book on the Peasant War can serve very well to illustrate this assessment.

The historiographic and theoretical significance of *The Peasant War* is, however, only one of the aspects which may make this discussion relevant for students of peasant societies. The relationship of peasants to other social classes and groups, the organization of resistance and revolt, the role of ideologies—particularly of religious ones—in peasant uprisings, the question of spontaneous rebellion *vs.* consciously prepared and led peasant war and that of leadership are all subjects that have been analysed by Engels and are still very much in the centre of scholarly and political interest. Some of these will be discussed below, but many more could be.

**Department of History, University of British Columbia.*

'The Peasant War in Germany': a classic of historical writing

First the historiographical question. It would lead far into nineteenth and twentieth century intellectual history were we to discuss the fate of Engel's book in the context of historical scholarship since 1850. It may suffice to say that *The Peasant War* has been little read and little discussed outside of Marxist historical schools. Its most recent renascence was marked by the extensive studies devoted to it in the German Democratic Republic during the last fifteen years. These in turn induced West German historians, motivated by both scholarly interest and the development of political relations between the two Germanies, to discuss its merits. The main stages of these discussions are summarized by Rainer Wohlfeil (below, pp. 98-103) and Günter Vogler (pp. 108-117).

The reasons for this limited and 'one-sided' (*ibid.* : *xxviii*) revival are manifold. For one, most historians of the early sixteenth century may have preferred to use the more informative traditional monographs, such as the one by Wilhelm Zimmermann (1841-43), which actually served as the basis of information for Engels' analysis. True, Zimmermann and several more recent books [cf. *Engels 1967* : *xli n. 48*] contain more details, but the belief that they are more 'objective' than Engels' may be treacherous. As to Zimmermann, his intention was, in his own words (1844): 'I wanted to give my people a book ... that would have relevant reference to the present: the great movement of 1525 is connected with the aspirations and upheavals of our times as closely as ... the day before yesterday with today' [*Friesen, 1973* : *9*]. It has recently been demonstrated that Zimmermann wrote his book in a missionary spirit and was convinced that by producing his monograph he was working hand in hand with the spirit of the times toward an immediate inauguration of the Kingdom of God [*Friesen, 1973* : *107-116*][1].

Still, for information on the events and their details one does best to turn to the more recent handbooks and scholarly monographs and not to Engels; his analysis has claims to significance other than that of being an exhaustive reference book.

In the critical introduction to his edition of *The Peasant War* Leonard Krieger listed three factors which in the eyes of a non-Marxist historian justify the inclusion of Engels' book in a series of Classic European Historians:

> 'First, it initiated a prominent tradition of socialist history on the era of the Peasant War, running through Karl Kautsky (*1895*), E. Belfort Bax (*1899*), and Roy Pascal (*1933*), to the current official Marxist studies. It is a tradition serious enough ... to rival the non-Marxist tradition and to leave the interpretation of the Peasant War still moot between them. It should be added, as a subordinate consideration, that the Marxist line is not only becoming more respectable academically but has always been more convenient scholastically. Of the historical works devoted wholly or mainly to the Peasants' War,

the only ones in English are those from the socialist tradition. The best of the non-Marxist tradition, old and new alike, remain in their original German. This tradition is available in English only through more inclusive works in which the Peasants' War is one topic among others.

'The second factor which warrants the attribution of classic status to Engels' *Peasant War in Germany* is more convincing, for it bears upon an essential and distinctive quality of the book itself. In the actual working out of his economic thesis through his religious material, Engels formulated relationships of practical interests to religious ideals that are more important for the connections they make than for the putative economic primacy from which he began. Undoubtedly, Engels' early religious experience and his lifelong conviction of a kinship between religion and communism helped him to approach, in the context of the religiosity of the Peasants' War, as close as he would ever get to an integral relationship among the variegated historical activities of man. The connection between the radical sects and 'peasant-plebeian' classes—the connection that embodied Engels' most penetrating historical perception—remains the one definite relationship that has been accepted by historians on both sides of the Marxist divide. In general, moreover, even if Engels' priority of social interests and his one-to-one correlation of the other religious confessions with social classes have found no such acceptance, the relevance of the social dimension to the religious conflicts of the Reformation era is beyond cavil and the discovery of how this relationship actually worked remains one of the live issues for European historiography.

'Third, and finally, *The Peasant War in Germany* embodies Engels' Marxist dilemma in a form that can help every student of history to know himself. Engels himself unwittingly pointed out the lesson to be learned from the work in a later summary of the historical principles that had gone into it. When placed in juxtaposition these principles make explicit the fundamental paradox of history that Engels' work, unpretentious as it is, does exemplify. The paradox consists in the necessarily variant views of historical events taken by the men who made the events and the historian who re-creates them, and it is Engels' glory to have cast his Marxism into a sixteenth-century shape that makes clear the ultimate ambiguity of the historian's situation.

'Engels, on the one hand, understood the point of view of the men who made the long stretch of pre-industrial history, and he recognized their right to put their own stamp upon that history. Because these historical subjects viewed "thoughts as . . . developing independently and subject only to their own laws", and because the determination of this thought process by "material life conditions remains of necessity unknown to these persons", the men of the pre-industrial era constrain "every social and political movement to take on a theological form".

'On the other hand, however, Engels also fully recognized the right of the modern historian to read back into this same pre-industrial era the knowledge of the primacy of "material life conditions", although this is a knowledge that only the industrialism of the historian's own age made possible. The historian need only perform this reinterpretation, as Engels felt he himself had, and what had been "the riddle" of the driving forces of history is thereby solved for all preceding periods as well as for his own. Needless to say, Engels remained too much of a Hegelian believer in the retroactive power of knowledge to have himself been aware of the problem posed by this combination of principles. But to others not so comfortably endowed his *Peasant War in Germany* will remain a case study in the problem of how far the historian can go in opposing to his subjects' interpretations of themselves contrary interpretations stemming from subsequently acquired knowledge which the subjects did not and could not have had about themselves. [*Engels, 1967, xi-xlii*]'[2].

Our discussion will concentrate on two points summarized above by Krieger. The first three contributions by German historians discuss the historiographical value of the analysis by Friedrich Engels, raising, however, several questions beyond the interest of the professional historian. The second part is opened by a student of the Chinese revolutions and takes its departure from the question of religion and revolution; no doubt, a crucial problem for both Engels and for everyone interested in the pre-industrial period and modern peasant societies. The comments of two social scientists from West Berlin, based on their field work and studies in the Middle East, are printed as a contribution to the discussion.

Engels and German Historians Today: The Question of Early Bourgeois Revolution

We are very fortunate and grateful to the authors that we can print three papers by major protagonists of the ongoing discussions in Germany. Rainer Wohlfeil was one of the first who made a number of arguments presented by his colleagues in the German Democratic Republic accessible to the Western public. His anthology of articles and his critical introduction to it [*Wohlfeil, 1972*] were significant steps in opening up the dialogue between the two Germanies. Ernst Engelberg and Günter Vogler have published extensively on both the theoretical and the strictly historical aspects of the subject (*see the references, below, pp. 123, 126*). Their willingness to participate and their kind assistance in the preparation of the English version of the papers made it possible to present for the first time outside the German-speaking world some of the main themes of this important scholarly controversy.

It is not unlikely that much of what is disputed in the opening paper may appear to readers trained in the social sciences as redundant hairsplitting over definitions, seemingly so dear to historians. And so might even parts of the replies. One may be, however, more patient with their argument, if one considers that while in Western Europe and the Americas the methodological framework of Engels *in general* has been for some time accepted by a wide circle of scholars as *one* of the possible dimensions of historical study [*Engels, 1967 : xl*], this was much less true for Germany. An analysis of this divergence would lead us far away from our immediate concerns. However, social and economic analysis as the *basic* approach to pre-industrial (and industrial) societies is still very much disputed among historians everywhere. Hence the opposing positions of the debate are relevant to more than just the German disputes.

Above and beyond the disagreement on the primacy of the socio-economic approach and the difference in the estimates of the relationship between the Reformation and Peasant War, the main controversy is about the quality of the events around 1525. This is actually also the question that promises to be of greatest interest for non-historians and students of peasant societies. The assessment of the struggles of the Reformation period as an early, immature bourgeois revolution, the first revolutionary attempt of European anti-feudal elements to overthrow the feudal society was in effect proposed by Engels (even if he did not use the words 'early bourgeois revolution', as Wohlfeil points out). An inquiry into the validity of this judgement is more than a question of definitions and certainly transcends the analysis of the revolts and rebellions in and around 1525 in Germany.

Vogler elaborates on the stage of development in the forces of production and social relations that prevailed in late fifteenth-early sixteenth century Central Europe and attempts to demonstrate that there were considerable elements of early capitalism present, at least in the urban sector. Several articles in this issue mention the late medieval agrarian crisis combined with manifold crises of authority and ideology of the old order. The growth of market relationships intruding into the village and the increased differentiation of the peasantry point to the beginnings of capitalist transformation in the countryside. The doubts of Wohlfeil about the 'bourgeois character' of the Reformation and even more so about that of the Peasant War are, however, not totally unjustified; there has not yet been enough detailed analysis of the economic and social bases of the period. Even Marxists tend to devote more attention to aims and ideologies, despite the programmatic words of Engels (quoted by Vogler, below p. 109), than to questions of land tenure, social conditions in the villages, market networks, changes in the forces of production etc. Recently, historians, both in the East and West, have been increasingly turning their attention to these problems; witness Blickle's article (above, pp. 63-74) and the works cited by him.

However, for those less curious about the details of the events around 1525 the main interest lies in the discussion of prerequisites, causes and consequences of this first (let it be granted, more or less) bourgeois attempt at the transformation of feudalism to capitalism. It is well known—and Engels' book is an analysis of the causes for this—that the peasant war did not lead to such a transformation and as far as the German states were concerned, neither did the Reformation movement. German societies of the sixteenth and seventeenth centuries were typical examples of the results of partial, half-hearted (in a word: truncated) bourgeois development, the reasons for which are too many to be discussed here. But students of modern peasant societies, from Latin America and Asia to the margins of Europe, are only too familiar with such truncated revolutions and pseudo-revolutions which left feudal and semi-feudal elements intact. For them, the study of that early, still immature bourgeois revolution that found its form in the German Reformation and the defeated Peasant War are of great interest. Engels' conclusions about 1525, which he augmented by comments based on the still uncompleted bourgeois transformation in late nineteenth century Prussian-junker Germany, remain, as Vogler puts it, 'valid as long as . . . there is an agrarian question' (below p. 109). The valuable arguments presented in the discussion papers and the many more in the books and articles referred to (see below, pp. 123-126) are of considerable interest to this general problem. It would, however, do good to widen the comparative and theoretical basis. For example, the 'myth of the *rivoluzione mancata*' (*Salomone, 1962*) about the truncated revolution of the Risorgimento in Italy gave Antonio Gramsci [*1949*] the departure for a profound analysis of the social and political conditions of pre-industrial Italy as an explanation of the many failures of the nineteenth and twentieth centuries. His paradigm for the reasons of the betrayal of a revolutionary peasantry by a weak and opportunistic bourgeoisie does not apply, of course, immediately to sixteenth century Germany or twentieth-century Latin America, but the relations of feudal backwardness and particularism to the immature forces of production and political struggle may offer useful parallels and fruitful comparisons both for theory and research.

Of course, the discussion around the revolutionary quality of the Reformation and its aftermath as well as its class character could be related in many other ways to studies of peasantries. It implies among others the question of class coalitions, extensively discussed by Engels both in the 1850 book and the later introductions. The view on the role of the peasantry vis-à-vis the workers or the rebellious elements of the ruling classes, e.g., the impoverished knights (as in the Sickingen discussion between Marx, Engels and Lasalle [*Engels, 1956 : 196-202*]), or the 'not-yet-ruling' classes, e.g. the burghers of 1525, may also serve as pegs for politically highly relevant inquiries into today's peasant movements.

Another aspect of the 'immature revolution' is the dilemma of the revolutionary leader in an early stage of social transformation. Referring to Thomas Muntzer, radical reformer and martyr of the peasant war, Engels wrote this splendid commentary:

> 'The worst thing that can befall a leader of an extreme party is to be compelled to take over a government in an epoch when the movement is not yet ripe for the domination of the class which he represent,

and for the realization of the measures which that domination implies
... Not only the movement of his time, but the age itself were not
ripe for the ideas of which he himself had only a faint notion. The
class which he represented was still in its birth throes and far from
being fully developed and capable of assuming leadership over and
transforming society. The social changes he fancied ... were little
grounded in the then existing economic conditions ... [*Engels, 1956*:
138, 140].

The ideological aspects of these words have been commented upon by
Greussing and Kippenberg (below, p. 128) but the questions of leadership and timing would be worth careful consideration. It may sound farfetched, but one might also keep in mind that the views of Wohlfeil and
Vogler and Engelberg about the peasantry in the transformation of outmoded social formations may, in the long run, have some impact on the
attitudes of their countrymen (and perhaps even their governments) to
societies where such transformations are presently on the agenda. Considering the increasing role of West German capitalist and East German
socialist involvement in the so-called Third World, it may be useful to read
the contributions with such contemporary ideas in the back of one's mind.

Although the main positions of scholarship in Germany, where these
issues are most hotly and expertly debated, are appropriately presented in
the three papers, we do not necessarily wish to close the discussion at this
point. Among others, Professor M. M. Smirin from the Academy of Sciences
of the USSR intended to add his comments to the discussion, but his recent
death cut short his plans. However, the *Journal of Peasant Studies* would
welcome further contributions to the discussion from anyone interested in
these questions.

Engels and Twentieth-Century Peasant Revolutions

The second part of the discussion is more clearly oriented towards the
present state of peasantries and peasant revolutions. We feel ourselves fully
supported by Engels in using his book as a departure for discussions
regarding peasant movements of the twentieth century, as he himself wrote
his work as a historical study for the understanding of nineteenth century
revolutions.

Neither the editors nor the contributors claim that a comparison of
Engels' conclusions with today's problems is their invention. It is true,
however, that the views of Engels 'are seldom referred to in Marxist
literature on the agrarian question' [*Sen, 1971 : 191*]. Explicit references
are indeed not too frequent. Lenin, for example, quotes Engels' *Peasant
War* only a few times, in connection with the role of religion in preindustrial societies and peasant movements. This, of course, should not
imply that he and many other revolutionary leaders of our time have not
been guided by Engels in their thinking about the agrarian question. Lenin
certainly valued highly his comments in disputes with the Narodniki, and

is the last who can be charged with not having understood Engels' words on the need for worker-peasant alliance (quoted below, p. 109). Regrettably, these warnings went rather unheeded in the socialist movements of Western and Central Europe.

'Surely it would be absurd to draw a parallel between the German peasant war of 1525 and Indian peasant movements' wrote Sunil Sen [*1971 : 197*] in the preface to his attempted class analysis of agrarian struggles in modern India. *Mutatis mutandis* this holds true for other areas of the world. Obviously, the peasants of Asia, Africa or Latin America of today (or yesterday) are very different from the serfs and small-holders of sixteenth-century Germany, even from the agricultural labourers of the Prussia of the 1870s to whom Engels referred in his later comments. Many papers in this Journal have been devoted to conceptualizing the special characteristics and particular problems of these peasant societies in comparison with traditional European peasantry. Still, the general issues raised by Engels seem to offer valid points of departure for a comparative analysis. A discussion on the Marxist views of most of the questions mentioned earlier, from leadership to alliance politics, would yield fruit. One of the central issues is, perhaps, the relationship of peasant revolts to traditional ideologies and social structures; religion and revolution may be the crucial theme in this context. The relationship between Lutheran Reformation and the Peasant War is obviously the most intriguing one for the sixteenth century German case and Engels' analysis is particularly sharp and enlightening on this point.

A comparison in a wider context has to consider the basic question of social progress *vs.* tradition under various conditions. Engels and, as we see in the first part of the discussion, many historians today see the events around 1525 in connection with the beginnings of the capitalist transformation of society, in which the forces of progress were rather unequivocally those of centralization and the strengthening of the state, the national market and the growing bourgeoisie. Different historical conditions in other periods and other countries would set the tasks of social progress differently. The stage of social disintegration in and around the peasantry may define the form, organization and programme of revolt and revolution in terms very different from those of late medieval Germany. Hence the 'model' of 1525, valid for much of Europe well into modern times (as Engels' comments on late nineteenth century Germany suggest), may not be applicable to twentieth century peasant movements, particularly to those outside Europe. This is the question to which Edward Friedman addresses himself. In his recent book he summarized his critique of modern social science, including Marxist revolutionary theory, in these words:

> 'With that communitarian change [that characterized the Chinese Revolutionary Party—JMB] . . . new, decent possibilities open up that members and defenders of the commercialized, endlessly innovative, atomized, materialistic societies can not easily permit themselves

to comprehend. Caught in the new individualized city world they often can not fathom those who have escaped to the old religious frontier community. Lenin misses the point when he identifies reaction with an allegedly culturally backward countryside. Marx misses the point when he criticizes revolutionaries for clothing themselves in the robes of almost mythic heroes. And Engels misses the point when he slights country people for understanding their rebellion in traditional religious categories. Believing that change, the bigger the better, is the essence of revolution, such people seldom see the value of return. But the promise of that egalitarian community toward which the Chinese Revolutionary Party almost despite itself took a halting, faltering step backwards is, and perhaps not only for traditional rural dwellers, revolution' [*1974 : 224*]³.

His present paper elaborates some of these points, with the Chinese revolutionary experience in mind, but not limiting his outlook to that. Friedman's suggestions of comparison between the 'two models', which he calls that of Engels and the Chinese one, go beyond the social and political aspects when he chooses to raise questions on the attitudes to life and death and the revolutionary world-view in twentieth century colonial and semi-colonial conditions.

The emphasis on the significance of the uprooted (pp. 121-2) seems to me particularly significant. It is true that Engels and many others in the revolutionary movement saw in the rootless 'lumpen' elements that exist on the margins of (more or less) industrialized-urbanized societies unreliable and dangerous allies for the revolution. But it is also true that uprooted people did play positive rôles in many pre-industrial revolutions, such as the beggars and vagrants in the preparation and propaganda of the later *Bundschuh* movements. Others, like early modern 'social bandits', hajduks and other non-peasants (Cossacks, Uskoks, etc.) supplied peasant revolts with valuable military experience and even leadership. Friedman's emphasis on the central rôle of the uprooted in Chinese revolutionary armies is a good example of the profound differences in social stratification and its consequences in terms of bases and aims of rebellion.

K. Greussing and H. G. Kippenberg were good enough to comply with our request for comments in the very short time limit we had to impose on them; they, like us, are aware of the incompleteness of their remarks, but we hope that they still serve as further incentives to a wider discussion. The two authors have based their contribution on both a critical assessment of Engels' work and their research and field work in Iran and Kurdistan. While they agree that Engels' studies have to be augmented by additional analyses of social conditions and ideas within the peasantry, they wish to qualify the possibility of 'return' to traditional forms of organization and sets of values in the course of resistance and revolutionary action. It is their contention that tradition needs to be transformed to be able to serve under the conditions of present day struggles. In the case of the Kurdish resistance movement in Iraq, which suffered a severe defeat recently, the task was to lift the limitation of tribal solidarity and reformulate its inherent solidarity, transcending the level of village or tribe into the consciousness of a national liberation movement. In Iran, where the land reform of the past decade has strengthened the bourgeois element in the village and left considerable strata of rural population dissatisfied, the task will be to dynamize the political and economic demands of the poor farmers: not in the flat sense of Western consumer society, but rather in connection with the wish for developing traditional forms of cooperation. Their analysis of the differentiation before and after the reform in Iran and during the struggle in Iraq suggests the intricate relations between internal inequality and feudal domination in the Middle Eastern countryside. Their comments on the Mahdist millenarian movements in Iran are aimed at demonstrating the specific characteristics of religious movements in offering a basis for new collectivist solidarities.

NOTES

[1] Naturally, it is tempting to equate this kind of utopian, millenarian view of history with the prognosis of scientific socialism about the final victory of a classless society. Friesen does not hesitate to do so and treats Engels' interest in the work of Zimmermann (and particularly the latter's view of Müntzer) as that of a fellow utopian. Thus the second part of his book (from Engels to Smirin) remains well below the level of the first, where valuable research is presented on the background of Zimmermann, a task which was long overdue and will be appreciated by all who wish to study the circumstances of Engels' writing the *Peasant War*.

[2] Reprinted with the kind permission of the author and Chicago University Press.

[3] Reprinted with the kind permission of the author and the University of California Press.

Rainer Wohlfeil*

There is hardly a book by a Marxist-Leninist historian about the age of the Reformation which does not refer to *The Peasant War in Germany*. Engels is regarded not only as one of the classical authorities for this period, but as the author of the fundamental thesis, according to which the Reformation and the Peasant War were stages of an essentially continuous revolutionary process. Together they represent an 'early, still immature form of bourgeois revolution . . . the early bourgeois (*frühbürgerliche*) revolution in Germany' [*Vogler, 1969: 704*].[1] It is considered to be the opening of a bourgeois-revolutionary transition from feudalism to capitalism, these two so-called social formations. Actually, the term 'early-bourgeois revolution' was not used by Engels.

Professor of History, University of Hamburg.

This is not the place to rehearse the origin, sources and historical significance of Engels' book, its 1850 and later editions, nor to discuss the plans of Engels for a new version, which he did not live to write. The reception of the *Peasant War* and its impact on socialist historians is another topic in itself. It should only be noted that Engels was well aware of the fact that a systematic history, based on the study of the sources, of the early sixteenth century from a Marxist point of view was still to be written. He saw his book as having an explicitly political-propagandistic function, and it was this 'exemplary unity of Marxist historiography and politics' that has been hailed by Marxist-Leninist historians [*Bensing, 1961 : 174*] and has lent the *Peasant War* 'an almost canonical validity' [*Nipperdey and Melcher, 1966 : 612*] and made it a model for all of Engels' followers. No doubt, the particular significance of this work was to a great extent due to the fact that the materialist view of history outlined by Karl Marx and Friedrich Engels had been for the first time applied to a period other than their own.

In contemporary German Marxist-Leninist historiography Engels' theses are regarded as 'the most important guidelines for the solution of the problems of the early bourgeois revolution in Germany', offering 'the best scholarly guidance for the presentation of this turning point in the history of Germany and also of Europe' [*Schilfert, 1953 : 370*]. This statement on Engels' authority defines the dependence of Marxist-Leninist historical writing on its classic model. It is the basis for the uncritical, and hence for the non-Marxist, incomprehensible acceptance of the ideas and judgments of Friedrich Engels. It is also the cause of the many difficulties Marxist historians face when discussing questions of analysis and assessment, which, due to intensive historical research, may suggest corrections of the 'classical' position. Additional problems present themselves when the theses of the *Peasant War* are compared with other relevant statements of Engels, which to a certain extent contradict them. These problems have recently been discussed among the historians of the German Democratic Republic with promising results.[2]

Engels drew the outline of the Marxist interpretation of the Reformation in the *Peasant War* on the basis of a somewhat simplified socio-economic analysis of the period. Compared with the general overview of Marx, this restricted treatment presents a rather narrow and flat view of history. Yet, Marxist-Leninist historians characterize it as an 'unsurpassed class-analysis' [*Bensing, 1961 : 193*], and accept it as a foundation for the thesis that the main opposing groups and their religious-political ideas, their 'ideologies', were basically defined by economic and social conditions. Hence the Reformation is perceived as a mass movement primarily determined by socio-economic factors and not, as by most other German historians, a process of intellectual and religious conflict and renewal. However, only the Peasant War was called a revolution by Engels.

The Peasant War has always been a very popular topic with engaged socialist historians, like August Bebel [*1876*], Karl Kautsky [*1895*] and

Franz Mehring [1964], who all followed Engels without adding new insights. Soviet historians turned early to the study of the peasant movements in sixteenth century Germany and M. M. Smirin [1955] placed them in the centre of his research on the period. He too followed the lead of Engels, but also considered the basic statements of Lenin [1963 : vol. 15, 43, vol. 35, 93-94] relevant to the subject. Still, Smirin, who has done extensive work on the sources, did not initially subsume the Reformation and the Peasant War under the category of early-bourgeois revolution in the manner which became generally accepted by the historians of the German Democratic Republic.

Their framework for the assessment of the period of the Reformation is contained in the 34 theses formulated by Max Steinmetz [1960] 'in the historical tradition founded by Friedrich Engels and renewed by M. M. Smirin' [1970 : 338]. A widespread internal discussion followed Steinmetz' theses whose first stage has been summed up in an 'intermediary balance-sheet' by Günter Vogler [1969]. The discussion is still going on, though less actively than in the first few years, and has 'by no means yet achieved the solution of even the major problems' [Steinmetz, 1973 : 99]. Most contributions have concentrated on the general assessment of the Reformation and the peasant war, i.e. on the evaluation of the historical events with reference to the revolutionary transformation of social reality. In the last resort they intended to adduce proofs for the dialectical, i.e. essentially deterministic, view of history in the Marxist-Leninist mold. Although several questions have been raised and re-interpreted, the official text-book version of the history of the period has not yet been affected by the recent discussions [e.g., Deutsche Geschichte, 1974]. It is, however, likely that the forthcoming publications for the anniversary of the peasant war [e.g., Illustrierte Geschichte, 1974] will reflect some of the new insights.

The currently accepted view is that 'the character and the origins of the Reformation were not ecclesiastical-religious . . ., [but] rooted in the general struggle for the renewal and reconstruction of the whole society in accordance with the wishes and demands of most of its elements, in which, of course, the theological-ecclesiastical reform movement played an ideologically leading rôle' [Steinmetz, 1969 : vol. 1, 16]. The Reformation and the Peasant War are seen as highlights in the history of the German people. They are to be recognized as integral parts of one historical phenomenon and not as isolated or loosely connected events.

The thesis about the 'early bourgeois revolution' did not, however, remain unchallenged. Both in the USSR and the GDR historians (e.g., Chaikovskaia [1956], Töpfer [1963, 1968]) voiced doubts. Although the critics are still to be heard, the protagonists of the original thesis carried the day. The prevailing view regards the Reformation as the first and the Peasant War as the second act in the struggle of bourgeoisie against feudalism, and both are inextricably linked in this revolutionary process. This thesis also governs the assessment of the world-historical significance of the Reformation, as the first outburst of bourgeois revolution in Europe, opening a revolutionary wave that introduced a kind of chain-reaction leading to the epoch of bourgeois revolutions. In this sense a European, even a universal, significance, is assigned to the Reformation, not for its theological and religious impact and the historical and political consequences of these, but rather in the context of Marxist-Leninist understanding of a world revolutionary process. Consensus has been achieved in several aspects concerning the assessment of the period. The major open questions seem to be related to the 'subjective and objective conditions [of the Reformation and the peasant war], their class character and their historical place in the transition from feudalism and capitalism both in the German and in the European context' [Vogler, 1969 : 704]. It is in relation to these issues that the question of the main task of the early-bourgeois revolution was raised. Steinmetz [1960 : 42-43] regarded the establishment of a centralized and unified state, together with the elimination of all feudal structures, as the central objective of such a revolution. Challenged by his colleagues, e.g. Müller-Martens [1961 : 86], Zschäbitz [1964 : 278 ff.], who maintained that the 'main task' was to enhance the development of early capitalism in the womb of feudal society, he accepted their arguments in his later works [1963 : 230]. As a result of these discussions the emphasis of the assessment has shifted from the struggle against particularism to the social aspects of conflict and the national question is now generally regarded as secondary.

Another characteristic discussion concerns the chronology of this 'revolutionary period'. At the outset it was dated from 1476 to 1535, and three phases were discerned. The first phase opened with the uprising led by the Piper of Niklashausen, whose considerable following suggested the beginning of a new type of peasant struggle. This period was characterized by a growing national crisis which entered its second phase in 1517 with Luther's posting of the 95 theses on the church door of Wittenberg. Thus began the early-bourgeois revolution proper, reaching the highest point and terminating in the battles of the Peasant War. In the last phase the cause of the Reformation became increasingly a matter of the princes, and the epoch closed with the defeat of the belated mass movements, such as the crushing of the Anabaptist utopia in Münster in 1535 and the execution of Jürgen Wullenweber, the leader of a group of radical burghers in Lübeck in 1537.

This chronology has been widely discussed and revised. Steinmetz [1973 : 99-100] now suggests a much shorter period extending from ca. 1470 to 1526. He argues that the Niklashausen movement is a less decisive starting point than the 'beginning of the capitalist era in Europe', which he dates into the last three decades of the fifteenth century. He also maintains that the defeat of the peasant troops in 1526 marked the end of a general revolutionary movement. Ernst Engelberg [1972 : 1285 ff.] again widens the chronology to an all-European series of dates: 1419 (Hussite Wars); 1453 (Fall of Constantinople, as an 'end of the Middle Ages'); 1517 (Luther); 1525-26 (Peasant War); 1536 (Calvin in Geneva). These chronological arguments, which cannot be pursued here any further, indicate the character of the discussions among the historians who base their judgements on the canonical acceptance of Engels. For those, however, who intend to compare the theses of Engels with the contemporary evidence, the questions of periodization, however interesting it may be, does not seem to be so crucial. They, like me, are much more puzzled by the question of how the Peasant War can at all be identified as a 'bourgeois revolution', and I have to admit that I am unable to perceive these movements as actions of the bourgeoisie.

Actually, the notion of the bourgeoisie in this context has been disputed even among Marxist-Leninist historians. However, it is puzzling that when Engelberg intervened in the debate, he admitted that it is 'a highly important question of research to establish the position of the bourgeoisie in feudal society', but added the categorical statement: 'whatever our judgment about the relationship between feudalism and the bourgeoisie, between the importance and size of the latter in comparison with the peasants, nonetheless, the bourgeoisie could not avoid the objective task of seeking a new social order and fighting for it' [*Engelberg, 1974: 171*]. This kind of position makes one wonder whether there is any concern by Marxist-Leninist historians to establish empirically the relationship between peasant war and bourgeois revolution. Certainly no proof of such a connection has been adduced so far. Nevertheless it is repeatedly stated that the Reformation and the Peasant War were bourgeois movements, solely on the basis of Engels' assumption of the possibility of a bourgeois revolution without a bourgeoisie. It is unlikely that historians not bound by the tenets of Marxist ideology will be convinced by the vague definition of a movement that is 'bourgeois in character'. I wonder, though, whether Steinmetz addresses himself to this problem when he writes that 'the studies of historians in the German Democratic Republic in the last fifteen years have not managed to prove conclusively all that we have proposed' [*1973: 101*]. To the outside observer it seems perfectly clear that many of the theses, statements and judgments on the period of the Reformation and the Peasant War as an early bourgeois revolution lack documentary proof.

All these critical remarks and doubts should of course not imply that it is not worthwhile to study and discuss these interpretative attempts, although many historians of the German Federal Republic have disregarded them for decades. However, discussion has to be based on an adequate knowledge of the axioms, theorems, categories and concepts of dialectical and historical materialism, without which there is no chance of a meaningful dialogue or clarification of the different positions. My attempts to open up such an exchange of ideas through the presentation of the conflicting views [*Wohlfeil, 1972*], and the comparative articles by other West German historians (e.g., the one by Thomas Nipperdey and Peter Melcher [*1966*]) have already attracted the attention of Marxist-Lenist historians. The present discussion may be another fruitful occasion for the continuation of the dialogue.

Returning to my opening points about *The Peasant War in Germany*, let me emphasize that the study of this classic is mandatory for anyone who wishes to participate in these discussions. The 'canonical validity' of Engels' book—even if not of every single statement in it—has been recently reconfirmed [*Engelberg, 1972 : 1286 ff.*], which makes it the more regrettable that no historical-critical edition has yet been produced. Such a highly desirable enterprise would have to clarify the relationship of Engels to his sources—above all to Zimmermann [*1841-43*][3]—and correct factual details by comparing Engels' text with the results of historical research since his day. The lack of such an undertaking suggests some of the problems in the attitude of Marxist-Leninist historians to their classic: they seem to prefer 'scholastic exegesis' [*Engelberg, 1972 : 1294*] to new, critical research. But, by doing so, are they not disregarding the counsel of Friedrich Engels himself who, in his letter to Karl Kautsky (1 February 1892), found it 'expressly necessary to prove from our point of view how very much the Reformation was a bourgeois movement' [*Marx-Engels, 1968 : vol. 38, 260*]?

NOTES

[1] It is worth noting that historians of the Peasant War anticipated the politicians by changing their terminology from 'early-bourgeois revolution in Germany' to 'German ... revolution' which corresponds with the spirit of the new (October, 1974) constitution of the German Democratic Republic.

[2] R. S. Elker [*1975*] commenting on the discussion between G. Vogler [*1972*] and E. Engelberg [*1972*] points out that 'the recent analysis of Engels' writings suggests the possibility of a significant differentiation between *The Peasant War in Germany* as a model of historical propaganda in the context of the social movement of the first half of the nineteenth century and the methodologically relevant statements of the late Engels, which may serve as guidelines for the research on the early bourgeois revolution'.

[3] G. Schilfert's unprinted Ph.D. thesis, *Engel's Schrift vom Bauernkrieg und die Quellen seiner Geschichtsauffassung* (Halle/S., 1948) does not solve these questions satisfactorily.

Ernst Engelberg*

The invitation of the *Journal of Peasant Studies* to comment on the paper by Rainer Wohlfeil, which contains several references to my article [*Engelberg, 1972*], offers me a very welcome opportunity to clarify some misunderstandings and to reflect on certain differences of opinion.

I should like to begin by stating that my article of 1972 did not deal with Engels' *Peasant War in Germany* at all. My interest was focused on those theoretical considerations which Engels began to entertain in the 1880s while planning to re-edit his book of 1850 on the Peasant War. The two basic themes upon which I commented and which I analysed originate there.

One of these is contained in the notes by Engels, jotted down in 1884 as a guideline for further elaboration: 'Reformation—Lutheran and Calvinist —is the No. 1 bourgeois revolution, the Peasant War being its critical episode ... Revolution No. 1, which was more European than the English

*Professor Emeritus, Academy of Sciences, Berlin. The assistance of Kathie Scardellato in the translation is gratefully acknowledged.—JMB.

and spread in Europe much more rapidly than the French . . .' [*Engels, 1956:222*]. The other passage, to my mind the second fundamental thesis on this subject, can be found in the *Special Introduction to the English Edition of 1892 of Socialism Utopian and Scientific*, where we read: 'The long fight of the bourgeoisie[1] against feudalism culminated in three decisive battles . . . The first was what is called the Protestant Reformation in Germany' [*Marx-Engels, 1970: vol. 3, 104*]. The second great upheaval occurred in England, and 'the Great French Revolution was the third uprising of the bourgeoisie, but the first that had entirely cast off the religious cloak, and was fought out on undisguised political lines' [*ibid., 107*]. Thus, Mr Wohlfeil's statement about Engels having used the expression 'revolution' only for the Peasant War (above, p. 99) is, as far as the 1850s are concerned, at least questionable, and, for the later writings, simply untrue.

The theoretical-methodological significance of the two statements is that the German Reformation with its apex and critical turning point, the Peasant War, were perceived by Engels as structurally connected and linked in a chain of development—both in the immediate and in the more general sense. This perception of the overall connection of European revolutions from the sixteenth to the eighteenth century permitted—even forced— Engels to simplify his terminology in order to present clear-cut contrasts. He uses bourgeoisie *(Bürgertum)* as a general term which is to be made concrete by the historical specification of its relation to time and space. Mr. Wohlfeil is, therefore, on more than one count unjustified in the charge that Engelberg 'intervened' (!) in the debate about the term bourgeoisie with the 'categorical (!) statement' that, in regard to the objective role of the *Bürgertum* in the struggle for capitalist transformation, 'no empirical proof is necessary' (above, p. 102).

Whatever one's attitude to Marxist historiography may be, no serious person can expect that empirical proof will be presented, as it were from scratch, in every single discussion. Marx and Engels are well known for their scrupulous empirical research and certainly cannot be charged with having speculated and theorized in the air.

Nor have Marxist historians refrained from doing detailed research in the last hundred years or so. Recently, a number of conferences have been held in the German Democratic Republic and several studies have been published on the historical problems of urban society and the development of the bourgeoisie.[2] These projects are to be continued and will be devoted to the changes in the burgher society and the economic, social, political and ideological transformations experienced by the early bourgeoisie. However important these changes may be, it would be a mistake to overlook the continuity: my point was and still is to emphasize the dialectical unity of these two aspects. As to the relationship of Reformation and burghers, it does not seem necessary to present the empirical proof 'from square one', as if historians, Marxists and non-Marxists alike, have not produced anything of value on these questions. The material available so far proves beyond doubt that the cities played a decisive part in at least the early stages of the Reformation. Two-thirds of the 180 or so known urban uprisings in Germany between 1518 and 1523 broke out after the Reformation (1521-23) and were directed against the Catholic clergy and Roman ecclesiastical institutions [*Steinmetz, 1975 : 258*].[3] Even after the defeat of the peasants, the urban Reformation grew well into the 1530s, independent of the Lutheran princes [*Lau, 1959 : 122 f., 130 ff.*].

The spiritual-religious and the socio-economic and political aspects of the Reformation are indeed distinct from each other while also closely interrelated, but this is not an 'either-or' choice, as Mr. Wohlfeil seems to imply, but rather a dialectically structured and dynamic 'as well as'. While it is necessary to distinguish between the impulses of the leading reformers and the motives of the burghers for the reception of the Reformation, it is no less important to take into account the mutual relationship between the reformers and the people. It is one of the ironies of history (as Hegel might have put it) that two men, so basically conservative as Luther and Calvin (the latter even more aristocratic), actually triggered a revolutionary subversion of the world. Whatever Luther's and Calvin's subjective intentions may have been, it was the bourgeoisie that primarily read and heard their words and was mobilized by them in Germany, in England, and in France. It is, therefore, ridiculous to repeat the polemical statement that Marxist historians postulate 'bourgeois revolutions without a bourgeoisie'.

Naturally, the relationship between Reformation and urban society needs further investigation, both empirical and theoretical. In my often quoted article, I wrote some years ago:

> 'It is a great contribution of Marxist-Leninist research on the Reformation to have demonstrated the four main groups of political-religious differentiation in the 1520s. However, two questions seem to be in need of further investigation. First, the organizational forms of the success of the Reformation in the cities; and second, the motives of the different strata of burghers, particularly the craftsmen and minor merchants, for their acceptance of the "new faith" ' [*Engelberg, 1972 : 1302*].

Such a research programme does not lend much support to the charge of negligence by Marxist historians of empirical research.

Let me add one more comment on the world-historical place of the Reformation. Mr. Wohfeil is mistaken when he maintains that Marxist historians assign a universal significance to the Reformation 'not for its theological and religious impact and the historical consequences of these, but rather in the context . . . of a world-revolutionary process' (above, p. 101). However much emphasis we may put on the Reformation and the Peasant War as the first link in a chain of bourgeois revolutions, no Marxist historian would overlook the various other aspects. Friedrich Engels was an avid reader of and critical commentator on the technological and philosophical writings of his time (Strauss, Feuerbach, Bruno Bauer), and knew very well what he meant when he used such an expression as 'bourgeois-plebeian movement in religious form' or when he spoke of a 'successful religious disguise'.[4] In one of the passages quoted in my article [*1972 : 1292 ff.*], Engels pointed out that the 'suppression of the Reformation in Germany would not have been a misfortune for Germany, but it would have been one for *the world at large*' [Engels, 1956 : 231]. This whole paragraph is actually a splendid example of the dialectical method of analysing the historical development of social phenomena in their different and often contradictory forms.

All these controversies are rooted, in the last resort, in the relationship between empirical research and theory. To begin with: there can hardly be anything like 'pure empiricism' in history, considering that all inquiry into the facts approaches the subject with a particular problem in mind, which in turn is defined by its practical purpose and the skills and knowledge acquired beforehand, i.e., basically by socio-economic parameters. An alleged 'pure empiricism' is less and less possible the further the process of the collective and individual perception of history progresses and the further the history of mankind proceeds.

The history of historical writing offers ample proof that the very questions that historians address to the material are to a great extent defined by their general preconceptions, which are in the last resort—more or less consciously—ideological. It seems advisable, therefore, that a self-critical historian should not propose to free himself of all ideology, which would be an illusory and futile attempt anyhow, but should rather assess the character and quality of his ideological position. Basically, the question in historical scholarship is this: which theoretically-founded methodology is best able to interpret and explain the structural process of development, based on facts gained from the study of the primary sources. In our times the choices seem to be between (a) essentially bourgeois German historicism, (b) basically West-European Positivism, and (c) materialist dialectics, which is in critical opposition to the other two.[5]

The wide fields of theory and method cannot be even outlined here, but so much needs to be stated that attempts at defining Marxist-Leninist historiography in categories of 'rationalism', 'one-dimensionality' or 'teleology' as done by, e.g., Thomas Nipperdey [*1967 : 256-57*] will never prove adequate. 'Rationalism', as used in this context, will fall short of understanding the dialectics between accident and historical necessity. The 'one-dimensional approach' simplifies Marxism to the point of equating it with an economic-technological view of history, and 'teleology' misses the dialectical relationship between causality and finality. In this sense, Mr. Wohlfeil's equation between a dialectical view of history and determinism (above, p. 100) is an example of the total disregard of the dialectics of history. Historical necessity, as expressed in the laws of history, is in no way identical with determinist inevitability. In general, one might expect even the opponents of Marxism to respect its theoretical framework (which, actually, developed from empirical research) and not try to impose thoroughly alien categories upon it, like the one mentioned above. If Mr. Wohlfeil is serious in proposing that fruitful discussions should be conducted on the basis of a good knowledge of Marxist-Leninist thinking, then it is not useful to describe this as a sum of 'axioms, theorems, categories and concepts' (p. 102). The emphasis on alleged Marxist axioms does not promise a successful elimination of mental barriers and prejudices.

Whatever attitude a historian may have to dialectical materialism as a philosophy and to materialist dialectics as a method, he should avoid charging Marxists with 'dependence' and 'being bound' if he wishes to enter a viable dialogue. Everyone, every social scientist and every historian, is socially dependent and ideologically bound in one way or another. No one can escape the dialectical relationship between freedom and restriction, independence and acceptance of authority, relative and absolute. The task is to handle these dialectical contradictions with care and courage in every scholarly enterprise.

And on this note let us return once more to the classics of Socialist thought. We do not know about a 'canonized' Engels—à la Nipperdey-Melcher [*1966 : 612*]—but we know of one, whose life, work, and thoughts deserve very special attention in the interest of scholarly research. Engels is indeed classic in posing challenging questions and describing essential structures and lines of development. The study of his method must be accompanied by the analysis of his theoretical statements on particular historical problems. Proceeding in this way, one will be constantly struck by the immense profit to be gained from reading his works, by the accuracy of his formulations when compared with the results of the intensive study of sources and, not least, by the fruitful impulses to be obtained for further investigations. The words of the 'classics' are neither to be 'believed' nor ignored: rather, they should be analysed in content, in form (their language, terminology, etc.), and in the context of their time and their subject matter. By doing so, this process may itself serve as a point of departure for new ideas and inquiries.

These marginal comments do not exhaust the subject raised in the discussion, but I hope that they may help to clarify some misconceptions and misunderstandings.

NOTES

[1] In the German translation of this passage—originally published in *Neue Zeit*, thus obviously approved by Engels—the word 'European' is added to 'bourgeoisie', cf. Marx-Engels [*1956 : vol. 21 : 104*].

[2] Most of the results were published in the *Zeitschrift für Geschichtswissenschaft*, e.g., by the group of B. Berthold-E. Engel-A. Laube [*1973*], with comments in the subsequent issues; W. Kuttner [*1974*]; and H. Hoffmann-I. Mittenzwei [*1974*], likewise with comments in the same volume.

[3] Cf. also *Deutsches Städtebuch* (1939–).

[4] Cf. the passages quoted in my article [*1972a : 290 ff.*]: many of these have been printed in the appendix to the recent translation of Engels' book [*1956 : 196–232*].

[5] I have dealt with this subject, too extensive to be discussed here, in an article [*1972*] and will return to it shortly [*Engelberg, forthcoming*].

Günter Vogler*

Since the French Revolution historical analysis of the German Peasant War has illustrated the close relationship between politics and scholarship. Thus the historiography of the period 1517-26 reflects to a very great extent political conceptions and controversies.[1] In the last few decades Marxist historians in the German Democratic Republic and elsewhere have done considerable work on this period. With the 450th anniversary of the Peasant War, the subject again became a focus of interest, both scholarly and political, and accordingly the views of Marxist-Leninist historians have received more attention. An expression of this upsurge of interest was the publication of two volumes of articles, edited by R. Wohlfeil, outlining the main questions of discussion [1972, 1975].

R. Wohlfeil's discussion paper in this issue, like his earlier summaries of the subject, starts out with the statement that the assessment of the Reformation period as an early-bourgeois revolution can be traced back to the works of Karl Marx and Friedrich Engels. He reports also that the discussions of the past fifteen years in the German Democratic Republic have led to new questions and new insights and have brought to the fore a number of problems regarding this assessment. However, he is inaccurate when he states that these 'theses, statements and judgement . . . lack documentary proof' (above, p. 102, also [1975, 10]). Both Marxists and non-Marxists have presented a considerable amount of historical evidence on the nature and character of the Reformation and the ensuing Peasant War. Historians of the German Democratic Republic have repeatedly encouraged detailed research into this period and, although much has been produced already,[2] such an enterprise cannot lead to final conclusions in a relatively short time. But I do not wish to embark on this question, which has been amply commented upon by Ernst Engelberg (above, pp. 103-107).

Without going into detail, it seems necessary to comment on the origin and purpose of Friedrich Engels' *The Peasant War in Germany*. Wohlfeil stresses that Engels wrote this work in the context of political propaganda (above, p. 99 and [1972: 11]). About this there is no doubt, as Engels himself stated in the introductions to the 1870 and 1875 editions. He saw the purpose of his articles as an analysis of the actions of the German bourgeoisie of the nineteenth century through a comparison with and critique of the events of the sixteenth century. It was also his purpose to clarify the relationship of the German socialist workers' movement to the peasantry and the agrarian question. In 1870 Engels wrote about the comparison of the two historical periods: 'Our big bourgeois of 1870 still act exactly as the middle burghers of 1526 acted . . . But even the proletariat has not yet outgrown the parallel with 1525' [Engels, 1956: 22-23]. While surveying the possible allies of the working class, he emphasized that the lessons of the Peasant War imply that

*Professor of History, Humboldt University, Berlin. Translated by John Black (UBC).

'... agricultural labourers form the most numerous class in the countryside ... it is the class nearest to the industrial workers of the towns, which share their living conditions, which is steeped even deeper if misery than they. To galvanize into life and draw to the movement this class ... is the immediate, most urgent task of the German workers' movement' [*ibid.* : *24-6*].

Of course, for Marx and Engels historical studies had the immediate purpose of political analysis and the enlightenment of the socialist movement. In 1856 Marx wrote to Engels that socialist victory 'in Germany will depend on the possibility of backing the proletarian revolution by some second edition of the Peasants' War' [*Engels, 1956 : 196*]. Their critique of Lassalle's view of Sickingen, in his drama on the Peasant War, belong similarly to the common ground of historical analysis and political discussion of class politics [*cf. Engels, 1956 : 196-202*]. To the end of his life Engels did not tire of emphasizing the need for socialists to 'go from the city to the countryside and become a power on the flat land' in order to achieve victory [*Marx-Engels, 1956 : vol. 7; 531*]. Marx and Engles' conclusions about the political significance of worker-peasant alliances are valid, so long as there exist feudal and semi-feudal relationships: as long, in other words, as there is an agrarian question.

Despite its political purpose it would not be justified, however, to limit the significance of Engels' work to its propaganda function; Engels, while pointing out that his work was not based on primary research, described the *Peasant War* as an attempt

'... to demonstrate the political constitution of the Germany of that time, the revolts against it and the contemporary political and religious theories, not as causes but as results of the stage of development in agriculture, industry, land and waterways, commodity and money trade then obtaining in Germany' [*Engels,1956 : 19*].

This attempt, i.e., the demonstration of historical materialism on a particular series of events, gave Engels an opportunity to create a conceptual frame of reference which can still serve as a solid basis for Marxist historical research. It is not its 'canonical validity' or 'uncritical acceptance' (as Wohlfeil put it), but rather its function as a scholarly impulse and point of departure for further studies that makes Engels' work highly relevant. An important additional step toward a Marxist analysis of the Reformation period was the investigation of the development of capitalism and of primitive accumulation by Marx in *Das Kapital*. It would lead us too far to recapitulate the most significant contributions of Marx and Engels to this field of study; perhaps it is sufficient to state that they laid the foundations for a comparative history of revolutions, in which the German Reformation and the Peasant War found their place as parts of a cycle of bourgeois revolutions.

Before discussing this question in some depth, I should like to add a word to the discussion on Mr. Wohlfeil's remark about Engels' having regarded only the Peasant War as a revolution. Ernst Engelberg has demonstrated (above, pp. 103-4) that if one looks at the entire oeuvre of Friedrich Engels it becomes clear how inaccurate this statement is. The bases of the assessment of the period were laid in *The Peasant War*, but Engels developed and refined his views in the following decades. The passages quoted by Engelberg, which could easily be augmented [*cf. Vogler, 1972 : 447 ff.*], prove this beyond doubt. The picture is thus much richer than Wohlfeil presents it. The crucial question is, however, how to look at the whole complex of the Reformation and the Peasant War as an early form of bourgeois revolution and how to define its place in the history of society.[3]

The Reformation and the Peasant War fit into three developmental processes, when understood as an early-bourgeois revolution. They were part of a wave of peasant uprisings and wars in several European countries from the beginning of the fourteenth century which receded only in the eighteenth. They were also part of the reform movement represented by Wycliffe in England and Hus in Bohemia. With Luther and Calvin it became a stimulus for carrying out reforms in many European countries and also had an impact upon the formation of revolutionary movements in the Netherlands and England. The Reformation and the Peasant War should also be seen in the context of the accumulation of capital and the development of capitalism. Together with other factors they both signalled the beginning of a new epoch: the transition from feudalism to capitalism. Seen from this developmental, Marxist perspective, the Reformation and the Peasant War take on a new historiographical significance.

In order to promote the expansion of capitalism and the growth of the bourgeoisie, it was necessary to overcome the limits on social progress in the cities and in the countryside. Political power had to be redefined to reflect the economic power of the bourgeoisie. The attack on feudal power was at first directed against the predominance of the Roman Catholic Church. The Church was one of the main props of feudalism, because of its controlling position in spiritual life, its extensive landholdings, and its political influence.

The struggle against the Church was not enough, however, to overcome the contradictions between social progress and political power. The feudal offensive in the countryside, which culminated in the efforts to strengthen feudal dependency and exploitation, operated against the early process of capital accumulation, just as did the attempts to preserve the old forms of simple commodity production, particularly the guild system. Any acceleration in the development of capitalism had as a precondition the elimination of these limitations. The political distribution of power had to be modified if economic and social problems were to be solved. Only in this way could the prerequisites for the development of a centralized state be secured, which in turn would reflect new economic and social needs. To do this the power of both secular and spiritual territorial authorities had to be broken [*cf. Vogler, 1975 : 19; Klassenkampf, 1974 : 145*].

The term 'early bourgeois revolution' implies class conflict, based on the contradiction between the feudal mode of production and aristocratic power on the one hand, and on the development of elements of capitalist production and the necessary changes in the political sphere on the other. The causes of the outbreak of class struggle in the form of the Reformation and the Peasant War are to be found in the economic upswing occurring as a result of the development of capitalism. This class struggle was fought with revolutionary means.

The capitalist burgher class was, however, only at the beginning of its development into the bourgeoisie [*Berthold, 1973 : 212; Vogler, 1973 : 1196*]. Its revolution occurred in a still immature situation; that is why it is necessary to add the limiting term 'early' to the definition of the events in early sixteenth century Germany as a 'bourgeois revolution'. There was on the one hand a rapid sharpening of contradictions demanding a revolutionary solution but on the other the subjective and objective conditions were still immature. This situation gave rise to the specific character of the revolutionary class conflict which took place.

I should like to concentrate on two questions. To what extent did these class struggles represent a revolution? To what extent did they reflect the class interest of the burghers, i.e. the early bourgeoisie?

First, the problem of revolution. Since the last decades of the fifteenth century various factors had revolutionized society [*cf. Illustrierte Geschichte, 1974 : 8 ff.*]. How the crisis affecting all important sectors of the society was to be overcome was at first an open question. Only after the failure of different attempts at reform did a revolutionary solution suggest itself. In analysing the factors that led to the revolution and the character of this upheaval, Marxists are not, as Wohfeil believes, 'adducing proof for the dialectical, i.e. deterministic[4] view of history'. The assessment of events in which the stake is the replacement of an outmoded social order by a new one demands, however, clarity about the character of both. The grounds for the describing of such a transformation as a revolution depend on the analysis of the specific stage of development of the class society under review. That is why we ask first about the preconditions which made a revolutionary movement become a revolution [*Vogler, 1974a : 397; Brendler, 1974 : 9 ff.*].

Revolutionary movements have taken different forms in the history of feudal society. From the beginning of the fourteenth century, for instance, various class struggles have occurred. Peasant resistance in Italy, Flanders, France, England, Bohemia and several German territories, as well as in Eastern and Southeastern Europe, erupted in peasant uprisings and wars of more than local significance. The demand for reform of both church and state grew all over Europe, and addressed itself more and more to the entire structure of the society. In many states a national movement was tied with this, manifesting itself, as for example in France, in a struggle against foreign enemies, but consolidated also in the struggle with the Roman Church. The various struggles and conflicts in the cities and between cities and feudal lords lasted throughout the fourteenth and fifteenth centuries. All these events should be seen against the background of the growth of towns and the development of medieval burgherdom [*Vogler, 1973 : 1189 ff.*]. However, urban growth did not yet signal the crisis of feudalism. Rather it belongs to a phase of class struggle *before* the beginning of the transition from feudalism to capitalism.

In our view it is characteristic of the early-bourgeois revolution in Germany that social, reforming and national movements combined into a higher stage, precisely under the conditions of the entry into a new age. Thus a social revolutionary movement emerged, which, if successful, promised strong impulses to the acceleration of the transition from feudalism to capitalism. The German early bourgeois revolution had many roots stretching far into the past, but in the last resort the social contradictions inherent in the development of elements of the capitalist mode production were decisive.

If we look back once more to the class struggles of the fourteenth and fifteenth centuries the differences between them and the situation during the early bourgeois revolution in Germany become evident. In several European countries the peasant class struggles had led to the abolition of serfdom or the relaxation of feudal relationships. This was especially true of the peasant risings in France and England. In several parts of Germany, however, the antagonism between the peasantry and the feudal nobility, as well as that between the peasantry and the cities, grew in the last decades of the fifteenth century. The cause of this was the attempt to bring the peasantry into even stronger feudal dependency. It was also as a result of the attempt to raise feudal rents and to use the market relationship in the interests of the nobility and the cities. This did not, happen, however, under the conditions of simple commodity production. Rather, these changes occurred during the development of the capitalist mode of production on a large scale which had direct impact upon the agricultural sector.

The failure of the numerous peasant conspiracies and attempted uprisings after 1570, as well as the inability of the ruling class to solve existing problems, established the preconditions for an extensive, variously motivated, peasant uprising. The insurgents wanted to break feudal ties, throw off feudal burdens, and abolish subjection to the many petty lords. In many cases, however, they went much further than this, to the point where they called for the end of feudal authority and the elimination of all feudal privilege.

While the reformation movements in several countries resulted in the accommodation of church and state to the changed social conditions, and gave impetus to the creation of national churches—and in Bohemia the revolutionary Hussite movement saw the first breakthrough in the struggle against spiritual feudalism—the German cities and territories remained largely dependent upon the Papacy. Thus a maturing large-scale, anti-Roman, reformation movement was able, under the given social conditions, to start a revolution and give it its class content. The form of the revolution was the Lutheran Reformation.

While the centralized feudal monarchies in other countries provide the national movements with a framework and the crown offered support for their further growth, the consolidation of the territorial states in Germany only increased the fragmentation of the country, and caused the failure of any attempt at a reform of the Empire. Social and political struggles were thus also connected with the aim of destroying the power of the princes who caused this fragmentation, and shifting the balance of political power in favour of the capitalist bourgeoisie. The widespread demands in the early bourgeois revolution for the strengthening of the internal market, the creation of a national church and consolidation of central authority point in this direction. The definition of this movement as a revolution arises from the fact that it was a conflict between two social orders, between declining feudalism and the initial stage of the rise of capitalism.

As to the question of the class character of this revolution: Wohlfeil observes that the historian who compares Engels' work with the source material finds a real problem in the question of whether or not the Peasant War was in fact a bourgeois concern. He is 'unable to perceive these movements as actions of the bourgeoisie' (above, p. 102). If one takes him literally, Wohlfeil seems to accept that there was a connection between the Reformation and the bourgeoisie but denies any such connection in regard to the Peasant War. Thus we turn our attention to a few features, which, to our mind, demonstrate the close connection between the Reformation and the Peasant War and show the bourgeois character of both.

The Reformation and Peasant War are united especially in their anti-feudal aims, even if the two phases of the attack can be differentiated in terms of their decisiveness and consequences. In the Reformation the attack was at first directed mainly against the feudal church, whereas in the Peasant War it was also aimed against the secular feudal authorities. The term 'anti-feudal aims' (*antifeudale Strossrichtung*) does not necessarily mean that bourgeois-capitalist progress was relevant, for there had been anti-feudal struggles and demands in previous centuries, without their raising the question of the transition from feudalism to capitalism. If we tie together these anti-feudal aims with the problem of the transition from feudalism to capitalism in the period of the Reformation and the Peasant War, we do this mainly because symptoms of crisis in various parts of society became evident in the last decades of the fifteenth century. These developed into a crisis of the entire society, and stimulated a fundamental change of social relations on a revolutionary basis. An anti-feudal revolutionary movement under the conditions of the gradual growth of capitalism necessarily tended towards the establishment of a bourgeois-capitalist society. In this way the bourgeois revolution became a social issue [*Steinmetz, 1965 : 392 ff.*].

The history of the Reformation makes this clear from the very first. Of course, Luther and Calvin also stood in the tradition of attempted church reform, but the Reformation expanded quickly into economic, social and political directions. This is evident not only from the numerous pamphlets, with their attention to manifold social problems, but is also especially conspicuous in the practical successes of the Reformation movement in many cities. While Luther's ideas did not at first affect the village, they deeply affected the burghers or their patrician city councils. Mostly under the pressure from the popular movement, steps were taken which decisively changed urban ecclesiastical life, and were not without impact on other parts of society.

> 'The parasitical role of the Catholic Church in the cities was largely abolished: the Church was integrated into the community, and subordinated to the community's councils. The monks and nuns were drawn into gainful activity. Monastic property was expropriated to the advantage of the urban bourgeoisie, and the clergy lost its old privileged position. Not only did the giving of alms, pilgrimages and processions lose their meaning, but also the numerous religious holidays were gradually reduced in favour of productive work for the urban population'. [*Illustrierte Geschichte*, 1974 : 173-4].

In this way the so-called 'inexpensive church' (*wohlfeile Kirche*) was created.

The secularisation of clerical property, the abolition of the special position of the clergy, and their submission to the jurisdiction of the city and to its taxes, the dissolution of the monasteries, the end of the tithe, the regulation of care of the poor, the restructuring of education—all these and many other changes corresponded to the urban bourgeoisie's interests, and, directly or indirectly, encouraged bourgeois-capitalist progress. In all these measures the position of the burgher society was strengthened, while the power of the old church and the feudal clergy was weakened. A major support of the feudal edifice had been badly shaken.

Despite the variety of disparate demands the Peasant War also challenged secular feudal authority. This could mean that only specific old rights were to be restored and certain burdens alleviated. But it could also mean that the ruling feudal authorities would be deprived of their power. The more radical interpretation is manifest in the articles about castles and fortifications which appeared in the programmes in the Black Forest and Upper Swabia as well as in the Tauber Valley in Franconia and in Thuringia [*Vogler, 1974 : passim*]. The course of the German Peasant War confirms that the demolition of the seats and symbols of lordships was taken seriously by the revolutionary forces.

Thomas Nipperdey and Peter Melcher [*1966 : 613*] suggest that Marxist scholarship, because of its inherent conceptual limitations (*Konstruktionszwang*), misrepresents the relationship between the bourgeoisie and the Peasant War. They, together with Wohlfeil, dispute several statements of Marxist historians both with respect to the rôle of bourgeois interests in direct relation to and interaction with the Peasant War, and with respect to the objective impact of peasant class struggles on bourgeois capitalist development. In our view, however, the question cannot be reduced to the relation of cities or of different urban elements to the Peasant War and vice versa.

The occasional objection that the term 'peasant war' is not appropriate because it covers neither the relevant problems nor the actual participants of the movement partly touches on this subject, for it draws attention to the question of how widespread the 1525 movement in fact was. To begin with, the movement of reform was carried on in and spread outward from the cities, while partially enhanced by the peasant uprisings. However, it could have developed independently of the cities as well. The break-through of the reformation movement to the countryside during the Peasant War is documented in the numerous demands in the peasants' articles for free election of pastors and for the preaching of the true Gospel. The struggles in the cities, directed against patrician governments, also continued. Part of the picture is the resistance of the small commodity producers to their inclusion in exploitative capitalistic relationships. Small merchants and traders opposed the large companies and their attempts to establish monopolies. Entrepreneurs in mining fought against the princes and feudal lords, and miners struggled for better working and living conditions. Socially critical literary polemic continued, and artists not only gave a humanistic view of man, which reflected bourgeois consciousness, its final form, but also showed sympathy for the peasants and their struggle. All of these things occurred during the German Peasant War. They were certainly not new occurrences in this period, but it is noteworthy how they stimulated each other.

Let us start with the principle that revolutions are fought in the interest of a particular class. In our case the events, subjectively or objectively, amounted to the smoothing of the way for capitalist progress, and the strengthening of bourgeois positions. The movement actually went much further than this, and undertook the destruction of the feudal order and the creation of social equality. This is a tendency visible in all bourgeois revolutions. Even if those who took up the pen or joined the armed struggle were not fully conscious of it, the tendencies embodied in their demands and actions were directed at what was possible to attain: the strengthening of the position of the bourgeoisie. In this respect many of the events of the Peasant War were objectively tied to the process of transition from feudalism to capitalism.

It is significant that in the first years of the Reformation many cities played leading roles. But once urban goals were achieved, the cities strove only to protect what they had gained. For them there was no question of a continuation of the movement towards further objectives. This extension of reform was, however, precisely the purpose of the groups who had not yet been able to reap fruit from the struggle. The differentiation in the revolutionary movement before the Peasant War was evident especially in the activation of the popular movement, and in the conception of a programme of popular reformation, as reflected in the views of Thomas Muntzer.

The Peasant War was in this way the most important movement of the Reformation, in that it expressed the problems of the social and political revolution.

It is in this sense that the Peasant War did not concern itself only with specifically peasant problems. Thomas Müntzer and Michael Gaismair were also concerned about groups other than peasants [Smirin, 1926: 295 ff., Bensing, 1966: 41 ff.; Macek, 1965: 353 ff.]. Recently the question of whether or not the interests of the 'common man' were at the centre of all this has been raised again [Blickle, 1975]. It is clear that plans for bourgeois reform, linked especially with the names of Wendel Hipler and Friedrich Waigandt, became part of the Peasant War. These amounted to the 'reformation of all lords and cities' in the spirit of an equitable and just society in town and country [Vogler, 1975: 80-6]. One cannot therefore deny that the demand for 'reformation' during the Peasant War took on a wider meaning than mere reform of the church. Even peasant demands show a connection with the development of capitalism. It is quite clear that the peasant uprisings occurred particularly in areas where there were developed urban-rural relations, areas of early capitalist production [Steinmetz, 1975: 257 ff.]. The realization of many of the demands raised by the peasants would have furthered the entry of capitalist elements into the village, including the development of 'capitalist agriculture', to use a modern term. If Wohlfeil speaks of the 'complexity of the Reformation' [1972: 23], we should like to apply the same term to the Peasant War.

Winfried Schulze has said that Wohlfeil's book [1972] offers 'the classic case of scholarly controversy between bourgeois and Marxist scholarship which can influence both empirical research and theoretical reflection' [1973: 252]. This view appears to us to be more promising than Wohlfeil's evaluation of the discussions of the past fifteen years as 'internal' (systemimmanent) and his charges that Marxist-Leninist historians pay more attention to the interpretation of their classics than to original research. The notion of early-bourgeois revolution is thoroughly based on empirical research, but it needs further testing and grounding in empirical and theoretical work. The problems, whether recognized by Marxist historians themselves or identified by their critics, encompass a whole programme of research, a natural manifestation of a healthy development of scholarship.

NOTES

[1] This has been clearly demonstrated e.g. by Steinmetz [1971: 347 ff.].
[2] Several bibliographies and bibliographical articles offer an overview of this output, beginning with Steinmetz [1960 and 1970], and continued by Volz-Brather [1975] and Hoyer [1974].
[3] The most recent treatment of the Reformation and the Peasant War from this general perspective can be found in the Illustrierte Geschichte [1974], summarized also in Klassenkampf [1974: 131 ff.]. The historical place of the Peasant War has been discussed in many articles published for the 450th anniversary, by Laube [1974 and 1975], Steinmetz [1975a and 1975b] and in my booklet [Vogler, 1975.]
[4] The arbitrary identification of dialectics with determinism is of course absolutely contrary to what Marxists mean by dialectical and historical materialism.

Edward Friedman*

In his analyses of the sixteenth century German Peasant War, Friedrich Engels developed a dynamic model of why peasant revolutionaries could not win power. Four centuries later in Indochina and Algeria, in Cuba and Mozambique, in numerous regions of the globe but, most importantly, in China, peasant revolutionaries did significantly better than Engels believed possible.

A polemicist might merely call attention to Engels' errors. A serious effort to understand peasant revolution, however, can fruitfully assume that flaws in Engels' shrewd model may usefully help us find some vital differences of twentieth century societal reality which have permitted a greater role for peasant revolutionaries. Engels' model leads us to deal with ultimate matters such as religion, subjective factors such as leadership, developmental questions such as centralization and strategic issues such as united front alliances.

To fight is to die

Engels treated insurrection as an art with rules. One should 'never play with insurrection unless you are fully prepared to face the consequences of your play'. Ruling groups torture and slaughter rebels mercilessly, massacring indiscriminately, including fellow villagers or members—even distant members—of one's family. Some people estimate that twenty million human beings died during the great nineteenth century Chinese peasant rebellion, the Taiping rebellion.

Understanding the open honesty of the rebel side, Engels' model brilliantly depicts them not as mere seekers of an end to economic exploitation but as people who long for obvious justice against brutal, cynical and illegitimate injustice. It was a combination of new taxes, burdens without authority, in a period where famine and death threatened, that cost rulers 'their aureole of sanctity' [Engels, 1966 : 52] and permitted rural folk to find in their cause the true, honest and just one. Need became both personal and ultimate. How else explain the willingness to risk likely death unless one discovers the larger cause which transcends ephemeral existence?

The local defenders, the so-called rebels, are opposed to ruling forces, which 'have all the advantages of organization, discipline and habitual authority'; the odds favour the power-holders. Rebels are most likely to lose; death is a probable destiny. With their numbers scattered, without common loyalty or natural shared leadership, these rebellions are inherently and invariably local. The rebel groups can, one at a time, be defeated or bought off or forced to retire from the field and return home. Isolated in their attempts, they are readily betrayed, discovered, destroyed and defeated. Given the odds and the likely outcome, people all too frequently abandon their rebellion and rejoin the rulers. Whence comes the twentieth century difference which impels more of these rural dwellers to fight on?

Integration into a world market can make agrarian crisis more of a

*Professor of Political Science, University of Wisconsin, Madison.

national phenomenon; rule of foreigners who have the technological and administrative power to suddenly centralize the state can make this crisis experience, these rebellions, far less local than Engels found. An enemy exists in common and is so perceived. Not the structure of the colonized peasantry as such, but their relation to a world system, facilitates a change from rebellion to national and nationalistic revolution. The increasing integration into a world market in the twentieth century increased dislocation, instability, cultural upheaval for the unprotected, marginal Third World peoples. Imperialism with its foreign rulers and foreign ways can facilitate a popular experience of older, shared, rooted cultural identities in opposition to foreign subverters of all that lends meaning to life. People rely more on familial, religious, cultural bonds: new religions grow, millennial rebellions explode.

Death and Revolution

To be sure, the new centralized state is also more powerful, more able to crush rebellion in the bud. This overwhelming likelihood of ultimate disaster does not merely indicate that successful revolutions are such an anomaly that no generalizations will comprehend them. (The improbable odds also call our attention to the need to confront the issue of death head on. The rebels do. But it is not so easy for modern societies where the young move on and the old die alone in hospitals and other impersonal institutions. We must overcome our cultural barriers and try to understand why people will throw their lot in with a movement which may auger one's own cruel and swift extermination.)

One must weigh most seriously Engels' notion that the language of the people was 'religious prophecy' [*Engels, 1966* : 72]. We can add Karl Marx's idea from his 1844 *Contribution to the Critique of Hegel's Philosophy of Right*:

> *Religious* distress is at the same time the *expression* of real distress and the *protest* against real distress. Religion is the sigh of the oppressed creature, the heart of a heartless world, just as it is the spirit of a spiritless situation. It is the *opium* of the people.

As Eric Hobsbawm has established, the larger changes responsible for this experienced crisis combining personal, familial and religious troubles can be dealt with in ways other than secular revolution, dealt with—albeit ineffectively—by social bandits, secret societies, new religions, etc. [*Friedman, 1974*]. Most important, a deeply ingrained and broadly based, traditional culture permits people to comprehend their choice not as life or death but as how to die, that is, how to signify their life. As members of social groups which are eternal, the pervasiveness of death in medieval Europe or early twentieth century China can combine with felt corruption of old spiritual leaders and a new nationalism, to help people find that their choice is to have their way of life destroyed or to fight against ultimate sources of the moral, personal and cultural scourge and thus reaffirm their way of life. Where the lack of marriage and children means death for one's way of life, fighting and risking death to change things, first and foremost one's identity, may hold the only promise for continuing life. As Engels' analysis suggests, a study of peasant revolution requires a comparative sociology of religion and traditional cultural integration and disintegration. It is probably most important for the high incidence and large scale of peasant rebellion in China that no centralized, state-related religion psychically tied peasant to ruler in a mentally moral manner.

Culture and Revolution

When the Chinese Red Armies set off on their 1934 Long March, much of China well knew that a great Taiping leader, Shih Ta-k'ai, had been forced to undertake a similar trek. In Shih Ta-k'ai's case it ended in death and destruction. Now the arch-enemy of the new revolution, Chiang Kai-shek, and his loyalists predicted that the Long Marchers would end up as Shih Ta-k'ai the Second.

Cornered, confronted with an impossible river crossing over a thin, open bridge guarded by enemy troops, the rural rebels of the twentieth century were reminded of Shih Ta-k'ai's fate in the nineteenth and vowed not to repeat it. When they, seemingly miraculously, fought their way to the other side, they spontaneously burst out: 'Long Live Shih Ta-k'ai!' In the pouches of the defeated bridge guards were messages urging the guards to do away with the rebels and make them Shih Ta-k'ai the Second. Because it followed on a legendary defeat, this victory, in Mao's poetry and in Chinese popular culture, turned the Red Army into an invincible army. In a traditional rural culture precisely because the first attempt ends in tragedy, the second need not end in farce. Rather, it can become an epic transcendence. Those who have no comprehension of the power of shared expectations of traditional rural culture to give life to vital and viable mentalities insist that the Long March was simply a defeat. The complex reality, however, is that the rich culture of China—and not just China—could turn defeat into a life-affirming promise.[1] The village young would be educated by song and story to models of how to act against unjust rulers.

Engels' questions concerned the peculiar traits of the German region. The peasants studied by him are not the peasants of England. Economic relations are infused by historical particulars. Medieval Europe does not exhaust all defining characteristics—size, unity of culture, state form, power of foreign enemies and invaders, etc.

The experienced African revolutionary, Amilcar Cabral, stressed these cultural differences between China and Guinea as elements facilitating or hindering mobilization and self-mobilization:

> 'The conditions of the peasant in China were very different; the peasant had a tradition of revolt, but this was not the case in Guinea and so it was not possible for our party militants and propaganda workers to find the same kind of welcome among the peasants of Guinea for the idea of national liberation as the idea found in China [*Cabral, 1969 : 50*].

The beauty of the Engels' study is that since he was so conscious that the region he was studying was different, his model facilitates others asking useful comparative questions about what too many dismiss as tertiary, superstructural superfluities.

Leadership

Engels' model, as a Leninist properly understands, puts tremendous stress on the indispensable leader making the correct decisions. One must seize the moment, move quickly, win victory after victory. But what is striking, in contrast, about liberation struggles in twentieth century places such as China or Mozambique is their protracted, convoluted character. One is reminded of the struggles of the Spanish guerrilla fighters against Napoleon's armies of occupation. People protested with arms everywhere. Bands formed. Some tillers fought part time. Patriotic young people threw their lot in with the cause. The elements for creating national armies grew.

What was unique about Mao Tse-tung was not just his military strategy —actually discovered and adopted independently by other guerrilla leaders such as Fang Chih-min and Liu Chih-tan—but his welcoming of and identification with traditional demands, unlike Engels and other modernists. One can contrast Mao Tse-tung giving funeral orations in villages and ordering his forces to give proper burials to all people on the revolutionary side (even in 1962, the Chinese army paused to provide proper burials for Indian soldiers who fought heroically against them), with Che Guevara in Bolivia robbing (and allowing to become carrion) the corpses of the first troops his guerrillas killed, an unfeeling, anti-religious act which disgusted and alienated Bolivian troops [*Gonzalez and Sanchez Salazar, 1969*]. As with the early years of the rural part of the Bolshevik revolution, Mao's not interfering with, but actually embracing and enhancing, local tradition permitted rooted people to turn the distant national leader into that saviour their legends, emotions and situations had long demanded [*Tucker, 1975 : lxiii*]. Engels' concern with millenarian yearnings can lead us, as it did not lead him, to the real demands of rural people. Not seeing how local insurrections could take on a national character, Engels insisted that what was local, religious and decentralized served rebellions but blocked real revolution. Identifying organization with reason, freedom and progress, he could not see genuinely liberating potentials in decentralized, physically powerful, semi-anarchistic forms.

Centralization and Localism

Only a centralized state, for Engels, could be taken by modern revolutionaries. A decentralized peasant society could not. In the latter, only the rulers had ties, resources and knowledge at the national level. In a centralized state the people would no longer be divided, isolated, mutually mistrustful. United, they would win. Surely the reality of millenia of centralized empire in China facilitated the common culture which eased mass national revolution. But that isn't the political centralization premised on a national market that Engels referred to.

Barrington Moore, Jr. [*1966*] has suggested that this centralization of a bureaucratic empire gives the state the power to deflect the rise of commercial classes and thus makes more likely a continuity of traditional peasant societies, capable of facilitating modernization with fascism (Germany and Japan) or with rural revolutions (China and Russia). But the foreign nature of the imperial enemy of such revolutions in Algeria, Guinea-Bissau, Indochina, etc., suggests not, as Engels argues, that the centralizers must win, but that the local traditions can find bases for joining people against weakened rulers, foreign or native ones, split against each other. Engels chooses to ignore his own massive evidence that people fought hardest for what was nearest and dearest to them, all the memories, dreams and sweat rooted in their own locale. The problem is how such local energies can serve the national cause and not, as Engels implies, how such localism must first be undermined by new, secular, modern, national identities.

Uniting with the Rootless

Engels' misunderstanding of the role of asceticism in the peasant revolution can lead us to his major contribution. He shows that this asserted principle of primitive equality is a symbolical, powerful way of demonstrating rulers are undeserving of their wealth. That is, a different legitimizing principle of distribution is put forward. All people, all working people, should divide the fruits of their labour. The rulers thus appear as exploiting parasites outside the bounds of proper human conduct, a kind of conduct especially in demand in bad times when the wealth of some clearly spells massive suffering, if not death, for hungry, landless others. The asceticism is an insistence that the sources of suffering should be brought to an end. In central China during the peasant uprising of the mid 1920s, the tillers tended to revenge themselves not on the biggest landlord but on those with wealth who let poor dependants starve in bad times.

This revolutionary asceticism, however, is not, as Engels claims, a renunciation of all pleasures. Too much imbued with the values of cosmopolitan and commodity society, Engels does not understand the true joys of cyclical celebrations (birth, maturity, spring, harvest, marriage, mourning) and popular festivities (dances, plays, story-telling, basketball, acrobatics, swimming, etc.), which are precluded when villagers are uprooted. The revolution in China is experienced by rural people, especially the uprooted, first and foremost as a return to such necessary and happy normalities.

Engels begins with prejudices against the uprooted. Lumpen, declassé elements were said to be 'the worst of all possible allies' [*Engels, 1966: 18*]. All his disdain for what was local, religious and peasant was linked to the uprooted. Tramps, vagabonds, beggars and non-organized day labourers could serve the armies of the princes or the peasants [*ibid.: 45, 82*]. Even in the peasant army they allegedly were the source of the lack of discipline, the fount of unreliability [*ibid.: 105-6*]. Yet he kept noting how defeated soldier remnants would join the rebel forces [*ibid*: *118, 120, 132*] and bring their military experience, a much needed resource [*ibid*. : *138*], how wandering Anabaptists contributed unusual courage and endurance on behalf of the rebellion [*ibid*. : *71*] while 'most of those who still had something to lose, went home' [*ibid*. : *105, 129*]. In conflict with his claims, Engels' evidence suggested that these uprooted people could prove the most militant of rural revolutionaries, and at more than a local or seasonal level. With no place to return to, they could fight anywhere, anytime. Their participation limits the importance of leadership or unique momentary opportunities.

As he rethought the question of peasants and revolution in writing a preface to the second edition, Engels began to pay more attention to the complexity of peasant society. He began to think in terms of middle and large landowners, small peasants divided into tenants and owners, some ruined by usury, and all different depending on the regional economy. Day labourers were no longer simply dismissed as lumpen elements. Rather, finding a way to draw their energies and discontents to the side of the revolutionary movement became its 'most urgent task' [*ibid*. : *21*]. Useless allies became necessary allies, Engels always insisting correctly that the tillers could never carry through the revolution to a successful conclusion on their own.

And just before his death, in considering the researches of Kautsky, he found 'only two considerable faults' with his understanding of *The Peasant War in Germany*. More work was needed to comprehend the positive role of those elements 'declassé, occupying almost the place of pariahs' and more stress had to be given to the impact 'of the world market' [*ibid*. : *9, 10*].

As is well known, the mobile armies of Mao Tse-tung based on these uprooted peoples, allied to villagers and deracinated intellectuals, and founding their strategy on an analysis of struggles for that world market [*Gittings, 1975*] can be comprehended as fulfilling that new project.

If it is true that the limited character of the early modern English revolution is related to the paternalist state aiding the uprooted and thus limiting their revolutionary potential [*Wallerstein, 1974*], if it is true that the conflict between tillers and uprooted in the great French revolution deflected some of that revolution's potential [*Lefebvre, 1973*] then the relation of the uprooted to the peasants' revolution is a most crucial one. Engels moved away from his original categories and began to inquire into this relationship as many Marxists today will not.

The members of China's Red armies had to discipline themselves, change themselves, to win the trust of rooted tillers. To be sure the trust and the alliance were never quite complete, but even in its partial form, as in its ties to local demands and patriotic aspirations, the revolutionary force thereby became more than the voice of a class or an economic segment. It became, more than most revolutions, the hopes and claims of a people, Frederick Engels' scholarly and political search—especially his openness to what didn't fit his ideological expectations—compels us to continue to rethink the requisites of such an integral, democratic society, and not just for the German people.

NOTE

[1] Reactionary manipulation of religious emotions as well as the irrationalities of fascism and racism readily lead revolutionaries to equate their project with universal reason, as if the issue were science against superstition. The twentieth century use of rational organization and scientific progress in Nazi death camps, Pentagon killing in Indochina and refined torture in too many places, when contrasted with the place of ethnic, regional and other similar group, irrational energies in the service of liberation, forces us to rethink the relation of unreason to revolution. This is not an either/or matter.

Kurt Greussing and Hans G. Kippenberg*

In the past fifteen years two different social processes for the transformation of peasant systems have become paradigmatic in the Middle East: the land reform in Iran which began in 1962 as the central part of the 'White Revolution' of Shahinshah Aryamehr and the Kurdish resistance movement in Iraq from 1961 to 1975. Both were focussed on the peasant class, which has been the *object* of the Iranian land reform and the *subject* of the Kurdish struggle. They have one common denominator which permits an analysis in relation to Engels' work: their context was that of bourgeois class development and the stabilization of centralized state power. That the Kurdish case was complicated by profound national conflicts should be noted.

Engels recognized that one of the main factors of the peasants' defeat 450 years ago was that they were 'scattered' [Engels, 1956 : 52]. He did not discuss the character of this disunity in depth but suggested that it was a consequence of poor social and political 'logistics', in spite of such exceptions as the Tyrolian movements, where Gaismair managed to unite the insurrection into 'a splendid campaign' [ibid. : 150]. If, indeed, lack of organization and unity were the main causes of defeat then they must have been rooted in the social conditions in the German countryside, particularly in the divergent interests within the peasantry. An analysis of differentiation within the village is, unfortunately, wanting in Engels' book. Most probably, Engels, who, as we know, had to rely on data supplied by Zimmermann, did not have sufficient evidence to allow such an analysis. A comparison of the theses of *The Peasant War in Germany* with problems of contemporary traditional societies points inevitably to these gaps and demands that, as Friedman suggests, we 'deal with ultimate matters such as religion, subjective factors such as leadership, developmental questions such as centralization' (see above, p. 117). We propose to look at some of these matters in the context of differentiations within the villages

*Institute of Iranian Studies, Free University, West Berlin. The assistance in the preparation of the translation by Polly M. Bak is gratefully acknowledged—JMB.

of the Middle East and shall try to exemplify them in the processes in Iran and Iraqi Kurdistan.

Mechanisms of Differentiation within the Village

Marx and Engels postulated for the Asiatic mode of production 'villages, each of which possessed a completely separate organization and formed a little world in itself' [*1953 : 102*]. This type of village was seen as the foundation of Asiatic despotism, the functions of which (finances, public works, military) were supported by the absorption of agrarian surplus. But the image of the localized and narrow-minded Asiatic village overlooks those very processes of differentiation within the villages which were actually stabilized and even intensified by the social organization of the expropriation of surplus.

The history of Iran demonstrates the continuous attempts of those who by delegation obtained the power to dispose of the surplus produce of the peasants to anchor their domination in the internal social organization of the village. From the beginnings of Arab rule onwards the institution of the tax contract *(qabāla)* contained such mechanisms. While the notables of the village were responsible to the government for the payment of taxes, they were able to raise more from the tax community than what they had to deliver [*Lambton, 1967 : 44*]. In this way the central authorities acquired a social link into the village by utilizing and strengthening existing social inequality for their profit. In the nineteenth and twentieth centuries the system of *gāvband* aided feudalism's invasion into the productive processes of the village. While land and water were usually the properties of the landlord and the peasants had to render dues in the crop sharing system for their use, the rural producers frequently owned a third factor of production: draught animals. For cultivation peasants joined in small workteams of 2 to 8 men *(boneh, sahrā, etc.)* and the owner of the oxen *(gāvband)* led the team and received for his role an additional share in the crop. Membership was often based on traditional rights, at least as long as kinship ties were part of the social system, otherwise teams were organized by the village leader as middleman of the landlord or the *gāvbands* themselves. These teams consisted mainly of peasants with traditional rights *(nasaq)*, while those without such rights *(khoshneshin)*, some 45 per cent of all peasants before the reform, had to find employment as agricultural labourers.

It is most likely that the different size of tenant lands developed from the differences in the ownership of draught animals; the larger holdings in turn stabilized the internal differentiation. From these factors a scheme of social stratification of the village can be constructed, as it has been done, e.g., by Niki Keddie [*1968 : 74 f.*].

Thus the Iranian feudal system worked on two levels: through the tributary expropriation of agrarian surplus on the one hand and through the ties of dependence among the rural producers on the other. The *gāvband* served as a guarantor of seigneurial interests, of stabilized property conditions and of rural productive processes at once. Favourite *gāvbands* of the landlord or his middleman received the better fields for cultivation and were able to operate mills, stores, shops and money-lending businesses; these privileges enabled them to control production and distribution in the village and to develop into a kind of village bourgeoisie.

Obviously, the extension of kinship relations still played a rôle in this type of Iranian village, but the factor of property became dominant. This transformation of village relations was closely linked with the organization of expropriation of peasant surplus by the landlords. Through an intricate system of land tenure and rental, the claims of the lord and the existing inequalities within the village were integrated into a productive process that in the last resort led to distribution of the crop between different owners. The co-operative system of rural production, in which the peasants were always dependent on each other, became an instrument of seigneurial manipulation.

In outlying areas, where integration into the feudal system decreases with the distance from the cities, institutions of collective work remain alive, without developing the inequalities they potentially contain. For instance in some Kurdish villages of Iran there are work-teams (*jūq*, literally 'yoke', from the Pahlavi-Middle Persian) which do not have the internal hierarchy described above. 'At the head of each *jūq* is a peasant known as the *sar* (head of) *jūq*. He has no special privilege, and is merely the oldest and most experienced or respected of the group' [*Lambton, 1969 : 300*].

In tribal villages mechanisms of reciprocity and equality often survive even after the external feudalization of the village. This seems to be the case in most of the Kurdish areas. The central mountain region of the Middle East where the Kurds live has traditionally been a marginal and refuge area in both political and economic terms. In the nineteenth and twentieth centuries processes of social integration produced several types of village which, due to their different social structures, display varied conditions for political action. There was the domination of weaker tribes by stronger ones who retain their structure but destroyed that of the vanquished in a kind of 'internal feudalization'. There were the villages which, while retaining their internal, tribal structure, became tributary to a landlord imposed by the central authority. Villages and village groups were feudalized by their own leadership, which either was assigned rights to tributary lordship by the state or acquired them in fights against the central authorities: in such cases kinship ties may still have been decisive in lord-peasant relations. Finally there were villages in remote areas where inhabitants were able to resist both domination by other tribes and control by the state [*Barth, 1953 : 18-66; Leach, 1940; Vinogradov, 1965*].

Integration and Revolution: Two poles of Transformation

The Iranian land reform and the Kurdish resistance movement signify two alternatives for the transformation of village constitution. Generally speaking they mean either the development of differentiation, with the aim of winning allies for the state power and the ruling group of the bourgeoisie, or the development of collective institutions of production and distribution with the purpose of mobilizing the (armed) peasants for the struggle for independence.

The Iranian land reform seems to have originated in a combination of two main factors: the ruling regime was forced to look for new allies against the aspiring professional middle class and at the same time had to cope with a growing financial crisis which could only be resolved with outside help. The political aspirations of the new middle class of teachers, students, engineers, doctors, etc., opposed the personalist rule of the existing system, because it was no longer compatible with their professional qualifications and status needs. Urban demonstrations and riots in 1960-63 were espoused publicly in 1961 by the National Front that had been outlawed since the fall of Mossadeq (1953). These internal conflicts were aggravated by the financial difficulties for which the regime needed US loans. The United States government in turn seems to have demanded a land reform as a prerequisite for assistance. Thus the regime decided 'that those classes whose members supported traditional patterns had to be strengthened and brought in closer contact with the political elite' [Bill, 1972 : 140], The 'White Revolution' as 'politics of system preservation' [ibid.] was clearly focused on those rural tenants with traditional rights to the land (nasaqdārs) whose tenancies were codified and registered as property in course of the reform (for details see Katouzian [1974]). The 'happy sitters' (which is the literal translation for khoshneshin), who had no such rights, were left out of the deal: about half of the peasants went empty-handed. Thus the registration of property meant the strengthening and codifying of the position of the gāvbands, i.e., of the rural bourgeoisie. They are the only group in the villages that has reaped economic fruits and is now in the position to participate in the capitalist transformation of the agrarian economy [Greussing, 1975].

Simultaneously, the reform destroyed the traditional forms of collective work pattern in the village. In this way the differentiation of the peasants into proprietors and non-proprietors was revealed, since the khoshneshin lost even those traditional share-cropping rights they might have had. Among the proprietors an additional split became apparent: between the economically powerful property owners and those who remained deeply in debt and have thus been excluded from economic progress. The khoshneshin have apparently totally failed to secure their claims and the small-owners, whose expectations remained to a great extent unfulfilled, constitute probably another centre of unrest [Bill, 1972 : 154].

While the Iranian process enhanced the potential inequalities in traditional peasant systems and made them into a lever of social engineering, the pressures of the Kurdish struggle in Iraq revitalized traditional relations that may have been alive only at the village level or even below that. In spite of the defeat that followed the agreement between Iraq and Iran (6 March 1975) the continuity of the struggle, its width and political unity bear witness to this. The material and human sacrifices demanded by the armed struggle, the care of the fighters, the wounded, the refugees and the cadres have been borne by the armed peasants and their families. These peasants had the choice of changing sides, as they had done frequently in past conflicts, but the recent struggles were based on an essentially peasant movement which succeeded in formulating its programme in terms of an interrelationship between traditional ideas and reconstructed institutions of social equality. Within the tribe during the fighting the movement returned to the original purpose of tribal relations: securing equality and united action. In order to sustain the struggle it was necessary to overcome the limitations of a kinship-based social organization and achieve an over-all equal distribution of burdens and rights; the Kurdish conditions demanded this and the political leadership to accomplish it. This kind of process thus restores the internal logic of such societies, without their particularist fetters. Tradition is retrieved in the context of understanding general societal relations and is relieved of that parochialism and narrow-mindedness which had been present in the development of these traditions [*Greussing, forthcoming*].

Backwards Towards Revolution?

Concerning the dialectics of tradition and resistance in peasant societies, we believe that one has to go below the surface to characterize the transformation processes in which peasant resistance is articulated in the recourse to traditional institutions and corresponding ideas. The political activity of resistance or even revolutionary action cannot be fully described by the notion of a recourse to a 'whole world' of the village, as if in a movement 'backward towards revolution' only the external conditions would need to be altered in order to resurrect rural collectivity and equality. This would be an unreal assumption, if only because of the fact that imperialism did not hit Asiatic societies in the state of chastity, but as a system which already contained at least elements of class domination down to the village level. Imperialism has been penetrating these countries through pre-existing contradictions, and using them as levers for introducing new social forms of communication, such as commodity production, centralized state control, rural transformations based on measures of social engineering ('rural development' programmes, land reform, 'green revolution' etc.) The oppressed peasants therefore cannot naively and directly call on the old traditions: elements of tradition can only be expanded in the new conditions. Basically, we find unsatisfactory a concept of rural social transformation, which emphasizes the unity of village life rather than the actual differentiation. There are two choices open for peasant societies in the Middle East: the development of the village community as an element of collective production on a national scale or the replacement of the collective structures of village work organization by private ones. As Marx wrote in his letter to Vera Zasulich, comparing Western development in the countryside to that of Russia, where capitalist transformation would mean 'transforming their common property into private property' [Marx-Engels, 1953 : 412], the choice depends on the historical conditions. This alternative became reality on the one hand in the Asiatic revolutions of our time and in the extension of private property following the Iranian land reform.

Functions of Peasant Millenarianism

Let us now turn to the functions of chiliastic (or millenarian) ideas in peasant societies, following Engels' lead, as these are also closely related to the alternative we have just discussed. Religion, as the expression of alienation in class societies, is necessarily replaced by revolutionary proletarian consciousness in the course of the development of bourgeois society or in brief: religion has to be *aufgehoben* by class consciousness. This view of Marx, spelt out particularly in his early writings, was shared by Engels. In the *Peasant War* he refers to this issue tangentially, when writing about some of the chiliastic ideas of the Taborites:

> 'Only in the teachings of Müntzer did these Communist notions express the aspirations of a real fraction of society. It was he who formulated them with a certain definiteness, and they are since observed in every great popular upheaval, until they gradually merge with the modern proletarian movement' [Engels, 1956 : 60].

And further: 'Just as Müntzer's religious philosophy approached atheism, so his political programme approached communism . . .' [*ibid.*: 71-72]. The parallels drawn here by Engels were founded in the social character of the German Peasant War. Although the protagonists of 1524-26 were furious peasants, they would not have been able to overcome their disunity without the alliance with urban plebeian elements. Thomas Müntzer, a representative of this plebeian leadership, had already realized and transcended the naïveté of peasant chiliasm. The urban plebeian class stood entirely outside society and was therefore not caught in its ideological tangles: neither in the feudal ideology and its counterpart the patriarchal dreams of the past, nor in the urban bourgeois critiques of the church:

> 'This explains why the plebeian opposition even then could not stop at fighting only feudalism and the privileged burghers; why, in fantasy at least, it reached beyond the then scarcely dawning modern bourgeois society; why, an absolutely property-less faction, it questioned the institutions, views and conceptions common to all societies based on class antagonism. In this respect the chiliastic dream-visions of early Christianity offered a very convenient starting point. On the other hand, this sally beyond both the present and even the future could be nothing but violent and fantastic, and of necessity fell back into the narrow limits set by the contemporary situation . . . The anticipation of communism nurtured by fantasy became in reality an anticipation of modern bourgeois conditions [Engels, 1956 : 59-60].

The millenarianism that gave wing to the anti-feudal struggle of the peasantry is thus seen in the context of plebeian ideas and interests as an anticipation of conditions that were still far beyond reach. This view of Engels implies that there is a necessary sequence from the patriarchal conditions through feudalism and bourgeois society to communism, which, if insisted on as an objective criterion of measurement, defines all peasant attempts at obstructing feudalism as reactionary, and on the other hand, all plebeian fantasies as anticipating the coming bourgeois development of the conditions of emancipation [*ibid.* : *58 ff., 138 ff.*]. Engels' formulation, by granting only to Müntzer's 'anticipation' an objective interpretation (as that of the proletarian element in the anti-feudal struggle) skips the historical experience of the revolutionaries and postulates the law of strict sequence of social formations. However, the revolutions of the twentieth century in Asia did not pass through the bourgeois epoch but proceeded by a shortcut (if that is the correct simile) from the pre-capitalist mode of production to the socialist one [*Kramer, 1973*]. It is therefore necessary to re-assess the function of peasant chiliasm in the alternative of non-capitalist transformation in a way that Engels did not pursue.

Mahdism in the Middle East

Babism in the past century demonstrated that some elements in Iranian religion acted as socially highly relevant ideas in the choice of alternatives for peasant societies. Briefly the history is this: in 1844 (= A.H. 1260) Mirzā Ali Muhammad, a *saiyid* from Shiraz began to preach a religion that spread quickly over Persia and erupted in a popular uprising in Mazanderan. The rebellion was cruelly defeated in 1849, the founder executed in the following year [*Browne, 1909*]. In order to strengthen his religious authority Mirzā had styled himself *bāb*, i.e., gate. This was a reference to certain Shiite ideas connected with the expectation of a chiliastic redeemer. Such beliefs, similar to the Jewish ones about a Messiah, were unknown to early Islam, as in *al-Kurān* only the second coming of Jesus is mentioned, and had been received only later into the body of theological tradition. Ibn Khaldun (d. 1382) in his *Muqadimah* collected the traditions (*haditt*) about the *mahdi* and scrutinized them for their reliability. Two themes were particularly widespread in these traditions: that the *mahdi* (= the one guided by God) is a decendant of the family of Mohammed and that he will restore justice [*Rosenthal, 1958 : 162-3*]. This expectation is common to all Muslims. Shiite groups—mainly centred in the Middle East—differ from Sunnites in so far as they identify the *mahdi* with one of the 12 imams (descendants of the prophet with the right to rule) who was hidden away at a definite date in a miraculous way. The last, the twelfth, imam communicated with the community through four intermediaries from his first (the minor) concealment in A.D. 869 for 70 years until his final (major) concealment. The date of Mirzā's appearance as Bāb, exactly one thousand years after the accession of the last imam—from A.H. 260 to 1260—enhanced the belief that the great concealment was over and the coming of Imam Mahdi was near [*Browne, 1975 : 332*]. Soon afterwards, Mirzā proclaimed himself to be the concealed imam (= Qā'im).

The proclamation of the return of the imam had its own political logic. His orders were to weigh more than those of the then ruling Kajar dynasty:

> Now His ordinances are esoteric ordinances, and when the esoteric comes, the exoteric order must needs depart. Thus it is to be understood from certain traditions that under the rule of Him who is to arise of the Family of Muhammad, men will go to the bazaars, invoke blessings, and take (as an equivalent) whatever they please from the shops; which thing should one do now, he would, according to the law of the Prophet of God, forfeit his hand. In short, the ordinances of the religion of the Ka'im (upon whom be peace) are the ordinances of Unity: all goods are His goods; all men are His servants; and all women are His handmaidens, whom He giveth to whomsoever He pleaseth, and taketh, from whomsoever He pleaseth [Browne, 1975: 357 f.].

It is obvious that in nineteenth-century Persia there was great interest in such an order, above all among the peasants and craftsmen who were hardest hit by the influence of European capitalism. The rural producers had to support the increasing consumption of the landlord and the state. The craftsmen were threatened by the competition of cheap factory goods. Under such conditions, the proclamation of the return of the imam and the abolition of the existing system were received as an act of liberation. The different ensuing uprisings were intended to make this promise real. The combination of the second coming and resistance had its roots in the centuries following the islamisation of the people of Iran. After the coming of Islam, head tax and the *kharāj* (dues in kind) had to be rendered in the same way and the same amounts as in the preceding Sassanidic era, and were mostly, as before, collected by rural nobility (*dehqān*). Only the final receiver of the dues had changed from the Shah to the Muslim community, represented by the Calif. If, then, there was a concealed imam who even had the power to send his emissaries to the community, then the claims of the calif lost their legitimation. The teachings about the return of the imam were thus from the very beginning connected with peasant resistance to the expropriation of rents by the central authority. This movement rarely reached the point of revolutionary action, but rather served to segment, its adherents retiring from the polity. Imamite groups grew and survived throughout the centuries, particularly in the peripheries such as the mountain areas and the Seistani desert, and managed to conceal their true beliefs from all outsiders (*ketmān*). They emerge in the annals of Iranian history as local uprisings and ethnic-religious resistance movements.

It may be said that the idea about the concealed and returning imam developed and spread in the period when Islam transcended its urban and nomadic original setting and penetrated peasant societies. The religious ideas of Islam did not exactly tally with the task of subsuming the village structures for the purpose of expropriation of rents. In the words of a Babi:

'Know, O people, that the amassing of wealth is antagonistic to the working out of faith' [*Browne, 1975 : 45*]. The Islamic religion of the Iranian people never became completely an advocate of the tributary form of social organization. The symbol of the returning imam is not that of a promise for a better order, but rather that of the end of all lordship. In the context of modern times it favoured social developments that enhance the revitalization of collectivist social and economic conditions.

These, like other ideas of redemption, play a significant rôle in social consciousness and its transformations.

> 'Such ideological movements provide the opportunity to imagine alternatives to present conditions, to experiment mentally with alternative forms of organization, and to ready the population for the acceptance of changes to come. They are mental rehearsals of revolutionary transformations' [*Wolf, 1971 : 61*].

The historical function of mahdism in the transformation of peasant societies is to sponsor a new type of solidarity beyond traditional loyalties, to propose a radical renewal of the world—not only the restoration of 'good old conditions'—and to integrate different groups into a social movement [*Hodgkin, 1970*]. Certain parallels to the function of 'divine law' in the German peasant war (see above, 54-60) are quite obvious.

Naturally this type of belief is not immune from being used as a legitimation of government power either; the present concealment of the imam may also serve to justify the existence of state domination. Here, too, it is the historical context that defines the trend of development and seems to have done so in Iran. However, in spite of the recent victory of the private over the collective elements, mahdism still remains—at least in the peripheral areas—an alternative in the potential revival of collectivist institutions and in articulating belief in an egalitarian and domination-free social system.

Conclusion

It seems to be a general characteristic of peasant movements that they interpret themselves in terms which do not take the actual social barriers to the movement into account. But this very fact may have lent dynamic to these movements and the ability to learn and struggle again, under new conditions which often emerged from the defeats.

Engels [*1956 : 20*] emphasized the need for analyzing peasant movements in the context of bourgeois class development and the growth of the world market. These developments, however, enter into correlations with existing rural differentiation and with village traditions that reflect this differentiation. Global developments change, of course, the conditions of peasant political activity, but the motivation for these actions often emerges from the immediate experience of social and traditional elements of village life and its contradictions. Any theory of political action that does not consider both external and internal conditions will remain barren; in the case of modern peasant movements this means an analysis of the differentiated reality of rural society.

REFERENCES

Barth, Frederik, 1953, 'Principles of Social Organisation in Southern Kurdistan', Oslo: *Universitetets Etnografiske Museum Bulletin*, VII.
Bax, E. Belford, 1899, *The Peasants' War in Germany*, London.
Bebel, August, 1876, *Der deutsche Bauernkrieg mit Berücksichtigung der hauptsächlichen sozialen Bewegungen des Mittelalters*, Brunswick.
Bensing, Manfred, 1961, 'Friedrich Engels' Schrift über den deutschen Bauernkrieg—ihre aktuelle Bedeutung 1850 und ihre Rolle bei der Herausbildung der marxistischen Geschichtewissenschaft', *Friedrich Engels' Kampf und Vernächtnis*, Berlin.
Bensing, Manfred, 1966, *Thomas Müntzer und der Thüringer Aufstand 1525*, Berlin.
Berthold, B. et al., 1973, 'Die Stellung des Bürgertums in der deutschen Feudalgesellschaft bis zur Mitte des 16. Jahrhunderts', *ZfG*, XXI, 196–217.
Bill, James A., 1972, *The Politics of Iran: Groups, Classes and Modernization*, Columbus, Ohio.
Blickle, Peter, 1975, *Die Revolution von 1525*, Munich.
Brendler, Gerhard, 1974, 'Von der Hussitenbewegung bis zum Aufstand in den Niederlanden: Zu den Vor- und Frühformen der bürgerlichen Revolution', *Jahrbuch für Geschichte*, X.
Browne, Edward G., 1909, 'Bab, Babis', *Encyclopedia of Religion and Ethics*, vol. II: 299–308.
Browne, Edward G., 1975, *The New History of Mirzā Ali Muhammad, the Bāb*, (reprint of 1893 ed.).
Cabral, Amilcar, 1969, *Revolution in Guinea*, London.
Chaikovskaia, O. G., 1956, 'Vopros o kharaktere reformatsii i krest'ianskoi voiny v Germanii v sovetskoi istoriografii poslednikh let', *Voprosy Istorii*, XII: 129–143.
Deutsche Geschichte, 1974 (3rd ed.), Hrsg. von einem Autorenkollektiv, 3 vols., Berlin.
Deutsches Städtebuch, 1939, Hrsg. E. Kayser, *1939, 1941, 1952, ff.*, Stuttgart.
Elker, Rainer S., 1975, 'Geschichtsforschung der frühen Neuzeit zwischen Divergenz und Parallelität', in Wohlfeil [*1975: 219–45*].
Engelberg, Ernst, 1972a, 'Nochmals zur ersten bürgerlichen Revolution und weltgeschichtlicher Periodisierung', *ZfG*, XX: 1285-1305.
Engelberg, Ernst, 1972b, 'Über Theorie und Methode in der Geschichtswissenschaft', *Probleme der Geschichtsmethodologie*, 11 ff., Berlin.
Engelberg, Ernst, 1974, 'Probleme der gesetzmässigen Abfolge der Gesellschaftsformationen: Betrachtungen zu einer Diskussion', *ZfG*, XXII: 145–73.
Engelberg, Ernst, forthcoming, 'Ereignis, Struktur und Entwicklung in der Geschichte', *XIVth International Congress of Historical Sciences*, San Francisco, 1975.
Engels, Friedrich, 1956, *The Peasant War in Germany* (also 1966, New York).
Engels, Friedrich (ed. L. Krieger), 1967, *The German Revolutions*, Chicago.
Friedman, E., 1974, *Backward toward Revolution*, Berkeley.
Friesen, A., 1974, *Reformation and Utopia: The Marxist Interpretation of the Reformation and its Antecedents*, Mainz: Veröffentl., d. Inst. f. Eur. Gesch.
Gittings, J., 1975, *The World and China, 1922–1972*, New York: Harper and Row.
Gonzalez, L. J. and G. A. Sanchez Salazar, 1969, *The Great Rebel*, New York.
Gramsci, Antonio, 1949, *Il Risorgimento*, Turin.
Greussing, Kurt, 1975, 'Politische Ökonomie des Dorfes im Iran: zum Verhältnis von dörflicher Klassenentwicklung und Landreform', *mardom nāmeh-Hefte zu Geschichte und Gesellschaft iranischer Völker*, 26–65 (West Berlin).

Greussing, Kurt, forthcoming, 'Soziale ind historische Determinanten des kurdischen Widerstands' in T. Zülch, ed., *Über die keiner spricht: Die 4. Welt im Aufstand*, Reinek bei Hamburg.
Heitz, Gerhard et al., 1975, *Der Bauer im Klassenkampf: Studien zur Geschichte des deutschen Bauernkrieges und der bäuerlichen Klassenkämpfe im Spätfeudalismus*, Berlin.
Hodgkin, T., 1970, 'Mahdisme, Messianisme et Marxisme dans le contexte Africaine', *Présence Africaine*, LXXIV: 128–153.
Hoffman, H. and I. Mittenzwei, 1974, 'Die Stellung des Bürgertums in der deutschen Feudalgesellschaft von der Mitte des 16. Jafrhunderts', *ZfG*, XX: 190–207.
Hoyer, Siegfried, 1974, 'Der deutsche Bauernkrieg als Forschungsgegenstand', *Wissenschaftliche Zeitschrift der Karl-Marx-Universität Leipzig*, 23, *Gesellschafts- und Sprachwissenschaftliche Reihe*, VI: 455ff.
Illustrierte Geschichte, see below, Laube, Vogler, Steinmetz.
Katouzian, Mohammad Ali, 1974, 'Land Reform in Iran: A Case Study in the Political Economy of Social Engineering', *Journal of Peasant Studies*, I: 2, 220–39.
Kautsky, Karl, 1895, *Die Vorläufer des neuren Sozialismus*, 2: *Der Kommunismus in der deutschen Reformation*, Stuttgart.
Keddie, Nikki R., 1968, 'The Iranian Village before and after Land Reform', *Journal of Contemporary History*, III: 3, 69–91.
Klassenkampf-Tradition-Sozialismus: Von den Anfängen der Geschichte des deutschen Volkes bis zur Gestaltung der entwick elten sozialistischen Gesellschaft in der DDR, 1974, Berlin.
Kopitzsch, Franklin, 1975, 'Bemerkungen zur Sozialgeschichte der Reformation und des Bauernkrieges' in Wohlfeil [*1975: 177–218*].
Kramer, Fritz, 1973, 'Kollektivwirtschftliche Ursprünge des Sozialismus in China und Russland', *Gesellschaftsstrukturen*, hg.v.O. Negt, 188–213 [Frankfurt].
Küttler, W., 1974, 'Zum Problem der Anwendung des marxistisch-leninistischen Klassenbegriffs auf das mittelalterliche Stadtbürgertum', *ZfG*, XX: 605–15.
Lambton, Ann K. S., 1967, 'The Evolution of the Iqtā' in Medieval Iran', *Iran (Journal of the British Institute of Persian Studies)*, V: 41–50.
Lambton, Ann K. S., 1969, *Landlord and Peasant in Persia*, London.
Lau, F., 1959, 'Der Bauernkrieg und das angebliche Ende der lutherischen Reformation als spontane Volksbewegung', *Luther Jahrbuch*, XXVI: 119–134.
Laube, Adolf, 1974, 'Der deutsche Bauernkrieg als Höhepunkt der frühbürgerlichen Revolution', *Geschichte und Staatsbürgerkunde*, Heft 11: 1000–1013.
Laube, Adolf, 1975, 'Der historische Platz des deutschen Bauernkrieges', *Einheit*, 12–30.
Laube, Adolf, G. Vogler and M. Steinmetz, eds. *Illustrierte Geschichte der deutschen frühbürgerlichen Revolution*, Berlin 1975.
Leach, Edmund, 1940, 'Social and Economic Organisation of the Rowanduz Kurd Kurds', London School of Economics and Political Studies (ms.).
Lefebvre, G., 1973 [1932], *The Great Fear of 1789*, New York.
Lenin, V. I., 1963 (5th ed.), *Polnoe sobranie sochineniia*, Moscow.
Macek, Jozef, 1965, *Der Tiroler Bauernkrieg und Michael Gaismair*, Berlin.
Marx-Engels, 1953, *Selected Correspondence*, Moscow.
Marx-Engels, 1956, *Werke*, Berlin.
Marx-Engels, 1970, *Selected Works in Three Volumes*, Moscow.
Moore, Barrington, Jr., 1966, *Social Origins of Dictatorship and Democracy*, Boston.
Müller-Martens, Eckhard, 1961, 'Zu den Aufgaben der frühbürgerlichen Revolution in Deutschland und der Rolle des Königtums' in G. Brendler, ed., *Die frühbürgerliche Revolution in Deutschland: Referat und Diskussionen . . . Berlin*

(Tagung der Sektion Mediävistik der Deutschen Historiker-Gesellschaft 21.1.–23.1.1960 in Wernigerode 2).
Nipperdey, Th- P. Melcher, 1966, 'Bauernkrieg', *Sowjetsystem und Demokratische Gesellschaft: Eine vergleichende Enzyklopädie*, ed. C. D. Kernig 1: 611–627 Freiburg/B (repr. in Wohlfeil [*1972: 287–306*]; Engl. transl.: 'Peasants' War' in *Marxism, Communism and Western Society: A Comparative Encyclopedia*, C. D. Kernig, ed., New York, 1973, 6: 238–247.
Nipperdey, Thomas, 1967, 'Die Reformation als Problem der marxistischen Geschichtswissenschaft' in D. Geyer, ed., *Wissenschaft in kommunistischen Ländern* Tübingen, (repr. in Wohlfeil [*1972: 205–29*]).
Pascal, Roy, 1933, *The Social Basis of the Reformation*, London.
Rosenthal, Franz, 1958, *Ibn-Khaldûn: The Muqaddimah*.
Salomone, W., 1962, 'The Risorgimento between Ideology and History: The Political Myth of Rivoluzione Mancata', *American Historical Review*, LXVIII: 38–56.
Schilfert, Gerhard, 1953, 'Zum Erscheinen des ersten Bandes des Sammelwerkes "Marx-Engels-Lenin-Stalin, Zur deutschen Geschichte",' *ZfG* I: 367–376.
Schulze, Winfried, 1973, ' "Reformation oder frühbürgerliche Revolution": Überlegungen zum Modellfall einer Forschungskontroverse', *Jahrbuch für Geschichte Mittel- und Ostdeutschlands*, XXII: 253–69.
Sen, Sumil, 1971, 'Dialectics of the Peasant Movement' in *Society and Revolution: Essays in Honour of Engels*, New Delhi.
Smirin, M. M., 1955 (2nd ed.), *Narodnaia reformatsiia Tomasa Miuntsera i velikaia krest'ianskaia voina*, Moscow.
Steinmetz, Max, 1960a, 'Die frühbürgerliche Revolution in Deutschland 1476–1535. Thesen zur Vorbereitung der wissenschaftlichen Tagung in Wernigerode...', *ZfG* VIII: 113–24, (repr. also in Wohlfeil [*1972: 42–55*]).
Steinmetz, Max, 1960b, 'Reformation und Bauernkrieg in der Historiographie der DDR', *Historische Forschungen in der DDR, ZfG Sonderheft* 142 ff.
Steinmetz, Max, 1963, 'Zu einigen Problemen der frühbürgerlichen Revolution in Deutschland' in G. Harig and M. Steinmetz, eds., *Lehre-Forschung-Praxis: Der Karl-Marx-Universität Leipzig zum 10. Jahrestag*... 222–238, Leipzig.
Steinmetz, Max, 1965, 'Über den Charakter der Reformation und des Bauernkrieges in Deutschland', *Wiss. Zeitschrift der Karl-Marx-Universität Leipzig* 14 Ges.-Spr. R. III: 389–96 (repr. in Wohlfeil [*1972: 153–62*]).
Steinmetz, Max, 1970, 'Forschungen zur Geschichte der Reformation und des deutschen Bauernkrieges', *Historische Forschungen in der DDR 1960–1970, ZfG Sonderband*: XVIII 338–50.
Steinmetz, Max, 1971, *Das Müntzerbild von Martin Luther bis Friedrich Engels*, Berlin.
Steinmetz, Max, 1973, 'Reformation und Bauernkrieg—Höhepunkte der Geschichte des deutschen Volkes', *Sächsische Heimatblätter*, XIX: 97–102.
Steinmetz, Max, 1975a, 'Der geschichtliche Platz des deutschen Bauernkrieges', *ZfG*, XXIII: 253–270.
Steinmetz, Max, 1975b, 'Zum historischen Standort des deutschen Bauernkrieges in der Geschichte der Bauernbewegungen beim Übergang vom Feudalismus zum Kapitalismus', Heitz *1975*: 27–47.
Töpfer, Bernhard, 1963, 'Fragen der hussitischen revolutionären Bewegung', *ZfG*, XI: 146–67.
Töpfer, Bernhard, 1968, 'Zur Frage nach dem Beginn der Neuzeit', *ZfG* XVI: 773–9 (repr. in Wohlfeil [*1972: 70–79*]).
Tucker, R., ed., *The Lenin Anthology*, New York.
Vinogradov, Amal, 1965, 'Kurd Cultural Summary', New Haven (ms.).

Vogler, Günter, 1969, 'Marx, Engels und die Konzeption der frühbürgerlichen Revolution in Deutschland. Ergebnisse und Probleme einer Diskussion', *ZfG* XVII: 704–17 (repr. in Wohlfeil [*1972: 187–204*]).
Vogler, Günter, 1972, 'Friedrich Engels zur internationalen Stellung der deutschen frühbürgerlichen Revolution', *ZfG*, XX: 444–57.
Vogler, Günter, 1973, 'Probleme der Klassenentwicklung in der Feudalgesellschaft: Betrachtungen über die Entwicklung des Bürgertums in Mittel- und Westeuropa vom. 11. bis zum 18. Jahrhundert', *ZfG*, XXI: 1196–1208.
Vogler, Günter, 1974a, Bäuerlicher Klassenkampf: Revolutionäre Tradition und historische Forschung, *Archivmitteilungen*, Heft 4: 123–125.
Vogler, Günter, 1974b, 'Revolutionäre Bewegung und frühbürgerliche Revolution: Betrachtungen zum Verhältnisvon sozialen und politischen Bewegungen und der deutschen frühbürgerlichen Revolution', *ZfG*, XXII: 394–422.
Vogler, Günter, 1975, *Die Gewalt soll gegeben werden dem gemeinen Volk: Der deutsche Bauernkrieg 1525*, Berlin.
Volz, I. H., S. Brather, 1975, 'Der deutsche Bauer im Klassenkampf 1470–1648: Auswahlbibliographie der Veröffentlichungen in den sozialistischen Staaten aus den Jahren 1945–1972', Heitz 1975, 573–603.
Wallerstein, I., 1974, *The Modern World-System*, New York.
Wohlfeil, Rainer, 1972, *Reformation oder frühbürgerliche Revolution?*, Munich.
Wohlfeil, Rainer, 1975, *Der Bauernkrieg 1524–1526. Bauernkrieg und Reformation*, Munich.
Wolf, Eric, 1971, 'Peasant Rebellion and Revolution' in Miller and Aya, *National Liberation*, London.
ZfG = *Zeitschrift für Geschichtswissenschaft*, Berlin (German Democratic Republic).
Zimmermann, Wilhelm, 1841–43; *Allgemeine Geschichte des grossen Bauernkrieges*, 3 vols., Stuttgart (several new editions).
Zschäbitz, Gerhard, 1964, 'Über den Charakter und die historischen Aufgaben von Reformation und Bauernkrieg', *ZfG* XII: 277–88 (repr. in Wohlfeil [*1972: 124–43*]).

For Product Safety Concerns and Information please contact our EU
representative GPSR@taylorandfrancis.com
Taylor & Francis Verlag GmbH, Kaufingerstraße 24, 80331 München, Germany

www.ingramcontent.com/pod-product-compliance
Lightning Source LLC
Chambersburg PA
CBHW070624300426
44113CB00010B/1646